WHAT PEOPLE ARE :

WE HAVE NEVER BE

Kean Birch argues that today's economy is not organized around the free markets of neoliberal fantasy but through a financialized system of corporate monopoly – a system neoliberals actually promoted in contradiction to their stated commitments to free markets. Along the way, he provides accessible introductions to the history of neoliberal thought, monetarism, the causes and consequences of ballooning public debt, the growth of internationally mobile capital, the relations between asset values and corporate governance, and the dire straits of individuals in our current debt economy. His conclusions suggest ways of making our economies more just and equitable that deserves careful attention from both scholars and activists.
Joshua Barkan, Department of Geography, University of Georgia, USA

Kean Birch has a written a fresh and fascinating account of the relationships between neoliberalism, economic power and crises. Cutting incisively through the accepted, but largely mistaken, nostrums surrounding neoliberal rhetoric and reality, his book makes a valuable contribution to understanding the continuing grip of a corporate elite on the global economy and the devastating consequences that flow from it.
Andrew Cumbers, Professor of Political Economy, Adam Smith Business School, University of Glasgow, UK

Kean Birch has written a book that is accessible to his target audience: young, inquiring minds wanting to know why this is happening to them, but not quite knowing where to begin looking for answers. This timely book is the beginning of an important conversation that today's youth must have about the practical possibilities for coping with the present economic crisis.

Eddie Nik-Khah, Department of Economics, Roanoke University, USA

Framed by an energetic and engaging prose, Kean Birch has written a compelling book that challenges us to reexamine what we think we know about neoliberalism. Much more than a mere volte-face to the contemporary tide of academic thought on the topic, Kean instead offers a deeply reflexive and appropriately provocative reassessment that brings the corporation back into view to demonstrate how neoliberalism is riven with contradictions that cannot be easily resolved by simply citing hybridity and process.

Simon Springer, Department of Geography, University of Victoria, Canada

Kean Birch tackles a key question of the moment: how should we, and how shouldn't we, understand the ubiquitous term of neoliberalism? Written in a clear and accessible style, that is often both amusing and angry, Kean shows that the current crisis cannot be understood when neoliberalism is understood purely in terms of a history of ideas, focused on the development, especially within academic economics, of a set of free market principles. Instead, he directs our attention to the structural transformations to the political economy in recent decades – transformations that often bear little direct resemblance to supposedly 'neoliberal' policy prescriptions. His discussion of the assetization of the economy is a crucial contribution to our understanding of the current conjuncture, while the key insight that the crux of these systemic problems is that we stopped taxing the rich and started borrowing from them should be the political slogan of the moment. This is an important book, and it

should be read by anyone concerned about constructing a progressive alternative to the destructive and dysfunctional politics of the present.
David Tyfield, Department of Sociology, Lancaster University, UK

We Have Never Been Neoliberal

A Manifesto for a Doomed Youth

We Have Never Been Neoliberal

A Manifesto for a Doomed Youth

Kean Birch

Winchester, UK
Washington, USA

First published by Zero Books, 2015
Zero Books is an imprint of John Hunt Publishing Ltd., Laurel House, Station Approach,
Alresford, Hants, SO24 9JH, UK
office1@jhpbooks.net
www.johnhuntpublishing.com
www.zero-books.net

For distributor details and how to order please visit the 'Ordering' section on our website.

Text copyright: Kean Birch 2014

ISBN: 978 1 78099 534 2

All rights reserved. Except for brief quotations in critical articles or reviews, no part of this book may be reproduced in any manner without prior written permission from the publishers.

The rights of Kean Birch as author have been asserted in accordance with the Copyright, Designs and Patents Act 1988.

A CIP catalogue record for this book is available from the British Library.

Design: Lee Nash

Printed and bound by CPI Group (UK) Ltd, Croydon, CR0 4YY

We operate a distinctive and ethical publishing philosophy in all areas of our business, from our global network of authors to production and worldwide distribution.

CONTENTS

Acknowledgements — xii

Introduction — 1

Chapter 1: Neoliberalism in Retrospect — 19

Chapter 2: Monetarism and Fiscal Prudence vs. Ballooning Public Debt — 49

Chapter 3: Corporate Monopoly and its Neoliberal Cheerleaders — 83

Chapter 4: Assetization and the Concentration of Economic Power — 116

Chapter 5: A Manifesto for a Doomed Youth — 151

Conclusion — 182

For Sheila and Maple

Acknowledgements

The ideas that form the basis of this book have evolved over several years, going back to the late 2000s. I have benefited from a very generous crowd of friends, family and colleagues during this time, all of whom, in some way or another, have contributed to my intellectual journey – whether they agree with me or not! I'd like to thank the following in particular: Andy Cumbers, Les Levidow, Danny MacKinnon, Matti Siemiatycki, Katherine Trebeck, David Tyfield and Geoff Whittam. More specific thanks are due to Benjamin Christensen, Sandy Hager, John F. Henry, Vlad Mykhnenko and Theo Papaioannu for their comments or help on earlier drafts. A big thank you is also due to my new colleagues in the Business and Society program at York University, Toronto; they and the students here have inspired much of my new thinking on this topic. Thanks also to my family, who, although now across two large oceans, always provide an enormous amount of emotional support. Finally, I owe most to Sheila, she is the reason I try and leave work early every day.

Introduction

Unlike in Marx's day a spectre isn't haunting Europe; it's a stumbling, rambling, mindless, heartless zombie we call *neoliberalism* and it's out to feed on our brains, wherever it can still find them.[1] Right now it's staggering around the Atlantic, rising from the grave in the United States and United Kingdom, then heading to Iceland, Ireland, and Southern Europe. Who knows where it'll head to next? All it wants is sustenance; it's had its fill of the best brains the world's had to offer for so long that now it is down to pitiful leftovers it's finding it hard to keep going.

But is this stumbling, incoherent monster really neoliberalism? Could it be something else that we've missed all along? These questions are what this book is all about. The book's title is deliberately provocative and polemical. Its wording pays homage of sorts to *We Have Never Been Modern* by the well-known French sociologist Bruno Latour.[2] The title is, however, about as far as I go in terms of drawing on Latour's work, at least here. What I focus on in this book is the mess the world has been left in after the global financial system blew-up in 2007-08. While many have waited for economic rebirth, the global financial crisis (GFC), as it has come to be called, has not turned out to be a simple tale of crash and burn followed by phoenix-like resurrection. Now, over six years later, we're still in the midst of it, even if it has morphed, or decayed slowly, into something else.

While the GFC may have started out as a financial crisis, it quickly turned into an economic one as unemployment and recession followed the collapse of the financial sector; this then became a public debt crisis as governments responded to these recessionary threats with massive stimulus packages and financial guarantees; it has settled, more recently, into an austerity crisis as politicians and policy-makers around the world balk at the very notion that they could try something new rather than turn back to "zombie economic" ideas – what many people now call neoliberalism.[3] There is little chance that these same political elites will challenge the powerful financial interests that got us into this state in the first place, even though the rest of us around the world face daily uncertainties of one sort or another, from losing our jobs to having enough food for ourselves and our families. Our ruling elites have shown their cravenness in the starkest of colours as they face off against the banks.

Now, whether neoliberalism is a zombie (or not) is not the focus of this book; others got there well before me. What I'm interested in is whether we can actually pin any of this on the stinking, decaying corpse of neoliberalism – was the GFC the fault of neoliberalism? Hence, what I'm going to do to start this book is problematize the notion that something we call "neoliberalism" caused the GFC. To do this I have to explain why I've bothered writing this book at all, especially as there are so many books, articles, documentaries and other works out there already, all providing their own take on the origins, causes, consequences, dynamics and so on of the GFC (see Box 0.1 for some suggested reading on this topic). I start with this in mind before providing a brief definition of neoliberalism and then outlining the rest of the book.

Box 0.1 Some Suggested Reading on the GFC

- George Cooper (2008) *The Origins of Financial Crises*. New York: Vintage Books.
- Graham Turner (2009) *No Way to Run an Economy*. London: Pluto Press.
- David Harvey (2010) *Enigmas of Capital*. London: Profile Books.
- John Lanchester (2010) *IOU*. Toronto: McClelland and Stewart.

- Nouriel Roubini and Stephen Mihm (2010) *Crisis Economics*. London: Allen Lane.
- Joseph Stiglitz (2010) *Freefall*. London: Penguin.
- Colin Crouch (2011) *The Strange Non-death of Neoliberalism*. Cambridge: Polity.
- Gerard Dumenil and Dominique Levy (2011) *The Crisis of Neoliberalism*. Cambridge, MA: Harvard University Press.
- Christian Marazzi (2011) *The Violence of Financial Capitalism*. Los Angeles: Semiotext(e).
- Matt Taibbi (2011) *Griftopia*. New York: Spiegel and Gau Trade Paperbacks.
- Yanis Varoufakis (2011) *Global Minotaur*. London: Zed Books.
- Mark Blyth (2013) *Austerity*. Oxford: Oxford University Press.
- Philip Mirowski (2013) *Never Let a Serious Crisis Go to Waste*. London: Verso.

Why Write This Book Now?

As I indicated above, I'm going to begin with why I wanted to write this book.

First off, it's not meant to be a summary of everyone else's arguments; that would be impossible considering how much has been written about the global financial crisis (GFC) in the few years since 2007 (and beforehand in some cases) – see Box 0.2 for a very brief outline of the GFC. I want to state quite openly and right at the beginning of this book that what I'm writing here is a polemic; it's meant to be provoke, it's not meant to be a dry analysis of things other people have written. I may be an academic, but that does not mean I want this book to be an academic treatise on the GFC or on neoliberalism. Nor is it meant as a critique of the numerous and various analyses of the GFC. What I aim to do is present a very particular and partial account of several topics I think have been overlooked or side-lined in both the mainstream and critical literature.

Box 0.2 The Global Financial Crisis

The global financial crisis (GFC) is not an easy thing to explain, or even briefly outline. The dominant narrative is that sub-prime mortgages in the USA blew up as the result of blow-back from overly complex financial instruments called collateralized debt obligations (CDOs) and credit default swaps (CDSs). Obviously this is too simplistic, but it captures the *catalyst*, if not *cause*, of the GFC. The Greek economist Yanis Varoufakis provides a detailed chronology of events from April 2007 until December 2008 which is worth looking at if you want an idea of what happened and when (Ch.6). In his book, he also discusses several people's theories about why the GFC happened, including: a failure of risk management; regulatory capture; outright greed; the culture of Anglo-Saxon capitalism; 'toxic' economic theories; and systemic failure (Ch.1). What Varoufakis argues is that the GFC resulted from a potent mixture of all these things, focusing on one over the other leads us to miss an important ingredient. I'll come back to a number of these things throughout the rest of this book.

Source: Yanis Varoufakis (2011) *Global Minotaur*. London: Zed Books.

A second thing to note is that I've found the concept of 'neoliberalism' – and apologies for the scare quotes, but it will become more obvious as you read why I've put them there – to be quite useful in my own work. In fact I co-edited a book with Vlad Mykhnenko called *The Rise and Fall of Neoliberalism* in which we define neoliberalism in fairly critical and, at the same time, orthodox terms (see Box 0.3). We were perhaps optimistic in positing the fall of neoliberalism, or whatever it is that has dominated the political landscape since the 1970s. By now it is evident that whatever happened during the GFC has not meant the end of this thing we call neoliberalism; whatever it is, it has not done the decent thing and slunk off the stage in shame at the trouble it has caused. Its continuing vitality – if not liveliness – helps explain why so many academics, commentators, activists etc. argue that it has taken on a zombie-like form – it is dead, in that it has lost its legitimacy, yet it still lives and, presumably, still stumbles around looking for more brains to eat.

Box 0.3 A Brief Definition of Neoliberalism

Neoliberalism can be defined as five key processes or policies:

- "*privatization* of state-run assets (firms, council housing et cetera);
- *liberalization* of trade in goods and capital investment;
- *monetarist* focus on inflation control and supply-side dynamics;
- *deregulation* of labour and product markets to reduce 'impediments' to business;
- and, the *marketization* of society through public-private partnerships and other forms of commodification."

Source: Kean Birch and Vlad Mykhnenko (2010) *The Rise and Fall of Neoliberalism*. London: Zed Books, p.5.

This leads me to the third thing I want to note; the ongoing financial crisis has been directly blamed on neoliberalism.[4] Quite a range of people, not just leftist critics, have laid the blame for the GFC at the feet of unregulated, free market capitalism. This includes mainstream politicians like the British Prime Minister Gordon Brown all the way to pro-free market commentators like Martin Wolf in the *Financial Times*.[5] At the same time, however, neoliberal or free market voices can be heard clamouring that the reason the crisis happened is because we were not neoliberal enough. A good example of this is Professor Philip Booth, editorial and programme director at the Institute of Economic Affairs (IEA),[6] who claimed in a 2012 interview that the "real cause of the crisis, especially in the United States was that the government underwrote people's reckless financial decisions". Interestingly he further argues that "[v]ery few people foresaw the crisis and how it would actually played out [sic]",[7] which begs the question of how people could tell their actions would be underwritten by the government before the crisis actually happened (i.e. they didn't expect a crisis so how did they know government would step in if there was one). What this sort of claim by neoliberals like Booth illustrates, however, is that it's quite difficult to identify and define neoliberalism let alone lay responsibility on it for the GFC since even the people we might call neoliberals, like Booth, disavow any suggestion that we were (or are) neoliberal.

Now, the fourth thing I want to note is that the blaming of neoliberalism for the GFC is where I intend to focus my arguments. Why? Well, financial crises are ten-a-penny around the world which raises the question of why this one has different causes (i.e. neoliberalism) than all the other ones that have happened (see Figure 0.1 below). What seems different this time is that the GFC started in and had its most significant impacts on what the late Peter Gowan called the *Atlantic Heartland* (see below); that is, primarily countries like the USA and UK which house the world's largest and most important financial markets.[8] Moreover, the GFC was a systemic crisis rather than an isolated crisis only involving one or two financial businesses or one country or region. This meant that its effects have rippled out around the world, with some of these effects still very visible and ongoing, especially evident in the European sovereign debt crisis.[9] Despite its global impact, the GFC has still been characterized as a crisis of Anglo-Saxon capitalism since this is where it was and still is centred, especially in the financial and housing markets that dominate these political-economies.

FIGURE 0.1: Banking Crises over the Last Four Decades

COUNTRIES (BY DATE OF CRISIS)	DECADE
Uruguay, United Kingdom, Chile, Central African Republic, Germany, Israel, Spain, South Africa, Venezuela	1970s
Argentina, Chile, Ecuador, Egypt, Mexico, Philippines, Uruguay, Hong Kong, Singapore, Colombia, Turkey, DR Congo, Ghana, Canada, South Korea, Kuwait, Taiwan, Morocco, Peru, Thailand, Equatorial Guinea, Niger, United Kingdom, United States, Mauritania, Argentina, Brazil, Malaysia, Guinea, Kenya, Denmark, New Zealand, Norway, Bolivia, Cameroon, Costa Rica, Nicaragua, Bangladesh, Mali, Mozambique, Tanzania, Lebanon, Panama, Benin, Burkino Faso, Central African Republic, Ivory Coast, Madagascar, Nepal, Senegal, Australia, Argentina, El Salvador, South Africa, Sri Lanka	1980s
Italy, Algeria, Brazil, Egypt, Romania, Sierra Leone, Czech Republic, Finland, Greece, Sweden, United Kingdom, Georgia, Hungary, Poland, Slovak Republic, Djibouti, Liberia, Sao Tome, Japan, Albania, Bosnia-Herzegovina, Estonia, Indonesia, Angola, Chad, China, Congo, Kenya, Nigeria, Macedonia, Slovenia, Cape Verde, Venezuela, Guinea, Eritrea, India, Kyrgyz Republic, Togo, France, Armenia, Bolivia, Bulgaria, Costa Rica, Jamaica, Latvia, Mexico, Turkey, Burundi, DR Congo, Uganda, United Kingdom, Argentina, Azerbaijan, Brazil, Cameroon, Lithuania, Paraguay, Russia, Swaziland, Guinea-Bissau, Zambia, Zimbabwe, Croatia, Ecuador, Thailand, Myanmar, Yemen, Taiwan, Indonesia, South Korea, Malaysia, Mauritius, Philippines, Ukraine, Vietnam, Colombia, Ecuador, El Salvador, Russia, Bolivia, Honduras, Peru	1990s
Nicaragua, Argentina, Guatemala, Paraguay, Uruguay, Dominican Republic, Guatemala, Iceland, Ireland, United States, United Kingdom	2000s

Source and Notes: Carmen Reinhart and Kenneth Rogoff (2009)

This Time Is Different: Eight Centuries of Financial Folly. Connecticut: Princeton University Press, p.346-7. Some of these "crises" indicate the failure of only one bank (e.g. UK, 1984).

This means, fifth, that when I refer to "us" or "we" – as in the book's title – what I'm referring to is this "Atlantic Heartland". Basically I'm writing about just three countries; USA, UK and Canada. Aside from their relationship to the GFC, the reasons I focus on only these countries is because of my own expertise – I know more about them than others – and also because I don't have space to go into the depth necessary to consider other countries. If you're interested in the diversities or varieties of "neoliberalism" then there is plenty of literature out there waiting for you to read, some of which I've highlighted in the endnotes.[10] What these three Atlantic Heartland countries share are comparable and similar political-economic characteristics, institutions and histories, as well as long-standing ties to one another. Thus I want to acknowledge now that what I'm arguing may not apply everywhere in the world; in fact it might make no sense at all for other countries. I have to leave this for others to argue about afterwards, however.

I've now come to the final thing I want to note and the central reason for this book. What I want to do in this book is pick apart two assumptions I'm finding increasingly problematic when we talk about the relationship between neoliberalism and financial crises. First, and as mentioned already, is the idea that neoliberalism *caused* the GFC; second, following logically from the first, is the idea that we were actually neoliberal in the first place. On the first of these, it is hard to support the notion that financial crises themselves are necessarily neoliberal; crises have been an endemic feature of capitalism since the 16th century as Giovanni Arrighi and others illustrate so wonderfully in their historical work.[11] In his book *The Long Twentieth Century*, for example, Arrighi showed how financial expansion and collapse are merely the "signs of autumn" – to use Fernand Braudel's phrase – of hegemonic world powers (e.g. Netherlands, Britain, USA). It is my conclusion from this that if financial crises – and *financialization* itself (see Chapter 3) – have happened before (and they have, repeatedly) then to claim that neoliberalism is *the* cause of financial crises now is surely to miss some critical part, or even the whole, of the story.[12]

However, my real interest is in the second issue, which is definitely in need of more justification and it is to this end that I'm dedicating the rest of the book. What I'll say here is that the thing I keep coming back to is an ambiguity that rears its head again and again. On the one hand, neoliberal thinkers, their theories, free market policies, and political-economic processes (e.g. privatization, commodification) are all supposed to promote and extend *free* markets (and hence political freedom); yet, when we look at the actual people, ideas, policies and processes that we generally identify as neoliberal, what we find is that they support corporate monopoly and the concentration and inter-dependence of economic (and political) power. This is a central issue because, as the heterodox economist Geoffrey Hodgson points out, nowadays most economic activity takes place *inside* organizations and not *within* markets.[13] It is this contradiction that I'm interested in examining in this book, the ultimate goal being to show that it is not *free markets* that underpin this so-called neoliberalism but rather a *free-the-monopolies* mentality and rationality. Thus the critical gap in existing debates and literatures I'm going to tease apart is how they ignore, or simply miss, the growing role of business organizations, especially large, multinational corporations, in our economies, the interdependence and concentration of economic power, and what this all means for the stability of our societies.

So, What is Neoliberalism?[14]

Before I go any further it is probably necessary to try and at least define what I and others mean by "neoliberalism" – this is, necessarily, going to be a partial definition since there is an enormous literature on neoliberalism. A lot of this has been written in the fairly recent past, especially since the year 2000, and it does not just relate to the global financial crisis.[15] Whether we blame neoliberalism for this crisis – as many do – or not, it is still important to identify and define what we mean when we use this term or we end up chasing ghosts; well, zombies. Luckily for me, there are numerous examples of people – academics and others – doing exactly that. What I am going to do here – if somewhat briefly – is outline some of the ways people – and they're mostly critics since the term "neoliberal" is now largely used pejoratively – have defined and characterized neoliberalism in all its glory. To me it is interesting that neoliberalism is used more by its critics than by its supporters, many of whom now classify themselves differently. This perhaps results from the contrast between critics trying to identify *the problem* (i.e. neoliberalism) and free market advocates (i.e. neoliberals) not wanting to pigeon-hole themselves or agree with one another on one perspective. This is why neoliberalism often ends up being used as a kind of background term to denote something bad – e.g. "neoliberal age" or "neoliberal capitalism" – rather than as a specific identifying thing. I am as guilty of doing this as anyone else.

I have to point out that, as a concept and term, "neoliberalism" is incredibly fuzzy; it has been used to mean a lot of things, mostly with negative connotations.[16] It is, therefore, difficult to know where to start with an exercise like this. Really, there are too many definitions of neoliberalism for me to cover; it is unlikely that anyone can come to any sort of sensible or single characterization of the concept. This is not necessarily a problem, however. What confuses things is that neoliberalism is used across popular discourse, in magazines, newspaper, blogs and so on (e.g. *Red Pepper, The Nation, Le Monde, The Guardian,* New Left

Project, etc.), as much as it is deployed in academic or scholarly debates. My personal journey has been an academic one, but I think it can be fruitful to draw on more than what are sometimes incredibly esoteric and arcane arguments when writing a book like this. Now, I've not reviewed everything there is to read about neoliberalism, so it is important to bear in mind that I can only provide a snapshot of an ever-expanding literature. However, that being said, I've still managed to read a significant proportion of the literature, and written about it,[17] so will give it my best shot.

A short and sweet definition of neoliberalism is that it represents a set of ideas and policies aimed at installing markets as the main mechanism for coordinating our societies. So, neoliberalism concerns the replacement of collective social action or political decision-making with individual interactions in (free) markets. I'll come back to the theoretical and ethical rationale behind this aim in later chapters. For now, it's helpful to note that neoliberalism is generally associated with the transformation of society and economy to institute these free markets. This generally comprises five processes or policies: privatizing government services, industries and other assets; liberalizing international trade and investment; controlling inflation and supply-side dynamics rather than stimulating demand; deregulating to 'release' business from impediments and to enable individual's to become more entrepreneurial; and the marketization of society through the introduction of markets and commodification throughout society. Obviously what I've outlined here is my – and my co-author Vlad Mykhnenko – own take on neoliberalism, and so others have different perspectives.[18] Others also contest the veracity and usefulness of neoliberalism as a concept that can help explain what has happened in different parts of the world.[19] I'll come back to this in the first chapter.

Should we worry that neoliberalism is a contested concept?

The answer is probably yes. My primary worry is that the fuzziness of the term means that "neoliberals" have found it all too easy to disassemble and deny their culpability for the havoc they wreak, especially because they can claim not to be neoliberals after all or that we are not neoliberal enough – see the Philip Booth example above. As a result, the ongoing criticism of neoliberalism might have had the perverse effect of obscuring precisely what it is we critics want to bring down by providing a free-pass to our targets. We are, thus, risking the continuation of those things we call neoliberal in our use of the term – perhaps imprecision has become our own worst enemy. What all this has meant is that I've become increasingly concerned about my own use of the term and have sought to dig down through the conceptual muddle to more and more precise definitions of not only neoliberalism but also other concepts like marketization – that is, the extension of markets into previously public- or state-run enterprises, organizations, etc. Consequently, I have started to explore in more depth the intellectual histories of neoliberalism in order to find answers to my questions. When did neoliberalism emerge? How? What has changed since then? Are we neoliberal after all? Etc. This has led me to more recent and growing literature on the evolution of neoliberal thought since the early- to mid-twentieth century which I'll come back to in the first chapter.

Outline of the Book

With all that in mind, what I want to do now is provide a brief overview of the different ways neoliberalism has been identified and defined in the academic literature. These definitions, which are all critical perspectives on neoliberalism, can be split into four groups. The first is about what Michel Foucault calls *governmentality*, which involves the rationalities and political technologies of neoliberalism.[20] This is about how the ideas of neoliberal thinkers like Friedrich von Hayek, Ludwig von Mises, Milton Friedman, Wilhelm Ropke, Lionel Robbins, etc. are entangled with particular political technologies of power. Here, however, there is an ambiguity related to what Philip Mirowski and others have called the "neoliberal thought collective"; although this collective includes thinkers, policy-makers and many others, the ideas emanating from the theoreticians coming up with free market ideas are actually rarely reflected in the policies enacted by politicians, at least in their pure form.[21] I cover this critical perspective in Chapter 1 where I explore the history of neoliberal rationalities and especially the changing attitude to (corporate) monopoly which, I argue, helps us to differentiate between earlier forms of neoliberalism and later forms of *more-than-neoliberalism*.

The second strand of research focuses on the influence of neoliberal ideas and morality; we could crudely call this the ideology of neoliberalism, although that would not really capture the complexity of the relationship between economics and morality. As people like Stephanie Mudge and Bruno Amable have pointed out in the journal *Socio-Economic Review*, neoliberalism is as much a 'moral' project as an intellectual one.[22] Consequently, it is important to remember that neoliberalism is a response to the fears many liberals had about totalitarianism in the early- to mid-twentieth century; this is exemplified by Hayek's 1944 classic, *The Road to Serfdom*.[23] What is notable about this strand is that neoliberal ideas do not always successfully translate into neoliberal policy; for example, monetarism is often identified as a quintessentially neoliberal idea, but it was a policy failure in countries like the USA, UK and Canada, and was abandoned shortly after attempts at implementation. This is the topic of Chapter 2 which focuses on monetarism and public spending retrenchment as specifically neoliberal ideas which most critics use to define neoliberalism, but which have not been successfully translated into policy. What I specifically want to illustrate in this chapter is how monetarism actually led to the massive expansion of public spending and debt, which contrasts with claims about neoliberals being anti-state or anti-state spending.

A third area of research is concerned with neoliberalism as a political or class project. It is most obviously associated with the work of Marxists scholars like David Harvey, Gerard Dumenil and Dominique Levy,[24] although it is not limited to these thinkers. Basically they argue that neoliberalism is a project to restore class power to economic elites and involves the reorientation of the finance sector to do so. While there is much to admire in this work, it is the strand of research that claims the most direct link between financialization and neoliberalism, which I've noted above is problematic in light of historical evidence. I cover these issues in Chapter 3 where I write about corporate monopoly and how neoliberals became cheerleaders for something (i.e. monopoly) that contrasted so sharply with their supposedly free market ideas and ideals. What this enabled was the concentration of financial assets and the creation of massive economic (and political) power in the hands of a few institutional investors and financial corporations – especially those deemed "too-big-to-fail". However, it's my argument that this results from long-standing corporate restructuring and drive towards corporate monopoly stretching back to at least the 1950s, rather than a class project.

Finally, there is a burgeoning literature on neoliberalism as a process – so, rather than a set of conditions or policies and their effects or outcomes, several critics argue that neoliberalism is more properly thought of as a process of neoliberalization. That is, as the extension of market-like rule through state power according to the likes of Jamie Peck and Adam Tickell.[25] While the process perspective avoids the ambiguities of trying to identify specific neoliberal people, ideas or projects, what it ultimately does is leave us with an empty chair when we want to lay blame. It is never clear who is responsible as almost anyone can be part of this process. In Chapter 4, where I discuss these issues, I also highlight how corporate monopolies and the concentration of financial and other assets can be better characterized as the *assetization* of society rather than neoliberalization. My aim in doing this is to identify those who might be responsible for the GFC by taking a meso-level perspective and looking at the role of corporations, as organizations, in creating the mess we're in right now.

What this brief run-down is meant to show is that neoliberalism is many things to many people. As mentioned, I'll come back to each of these four critical perspectives in each chapter, addressing one in each chapter as a means to situate my arguments. Before the Conclusion, I include a chapter on ways you – the reader – might contest the changes I identify over the last half century. This is Chapter 5, which I've very deliberately called "A Manifesto for a Doomed Youth" because it is directed at readers who are experiencing the worst effects of the GFC in the Atlantic Heartland, as well as further afield in places like Greece, Spain and Portugal where young people face crazy levels of youth unemployment. As a manifesto it is not a radical call to arms, to break down the barricades or storm the banks, it is rather – and intentionally so – meant as a more mundane programme centred on getting out of our entanglement in the current financial and economic systems.

1 The "zombie neoliberalism" trope is so popular that if you Google zombie + neoliberal you end up with over 4 million results.
2 Bruno Latour (1993) *We Have Never Been Modern*. Cambridge, MA: Harvard University Press.
3 In a recent book, John Quiggan identifies "the great moderation", efficient market hypothesis, dynamic stochastic general equilibrium, trickle-down economics and privatization as "zombie economic" ideas: see Quiggan, J. (2010) *Zombie Economics: How Dead Ideas Still Walk among Us*.

Connecticut: Princeton University Press.
4   Here I'll just reference two important examples of this sort of argument: Harvey, D. (2010) *The Enigma of Capital and the Crises of Capitalism*. Profile Books; and, Dumenil, G. and Levy, D. (2011) *The Crisis of Neoliberalism*. Cambridge, MA: Harvard University Press.
5   In the introduction and conclusion to our edited book, we highlight several of these claims: see Birch, K. and Mykhnenko, V. (eds) (2010) *The Rise and Fall of Neoliberalism*. London: Zed Books.
6   The Institute of Economic Affairs (IEA) is a free market think tank founded in 1955 by Sir Anthony Fisher, a businessman who was supposedly tasked by Friedrich von Hayek to found the IEA: see, Cockett, R. (1995) *Thinking the Unthinkable: Think-tanks and the Economic Counter-revolution, 1931-1983*. London: Harper Collins Publishers.
7   This was in an interview, available online: http://hungarianglobe.mandiner.hu/cikk/20121107_philip_booth_there_has_never_been_neoliberal_world_order
8   Gowan, P. (2009) Crisis in the Heartland: Consequences of the New Wall Street System. *New Left Review* 55:5-29.
9   See, for example, the likes of Blyth, M. (2013) *Austerity*. Oxford: Oxford University Press.
10 The following are just a small sample of the literature dealing with the varieties of neoliberalism around the world: Birch, K. and Mykhnenko, V. (2009) Varieties of neoliberalism? Restructuring in large industrially dependent regions across Western and Eastern Europe. *Journal of Economic Geography* 9(3): 355-380; Cerny, P. (2008) Embedding neoliberalism: the evolution of a hegemonic paradigm. *The Journal of International Trade and Diplomacy* 2: 1–46; Fourcade-Gourinchas, M. and Babb, S. (2002) The Rebirth of the Liberal Creed: Paths to Neoliberalism in Four Countries. *American Journal of Sociology* 108 (3):533-579; and,

Jessop, B. (2010) From hegemony to crisis?: The continuing ecological dominance of neo-liberalism, in Birch, K. & Mykhnenko, V. (eds.) *The Rise and Fall of Neoliberalism: The Collapse of an Economic Order?* London: Zed Books, p. 177-187.

11   Arrighi, G. (1994[2010]) *The Long Twentieth Century: Money, Power and the Origins of our Times.* London: Verso.

12   I've written more about this in a free, online working paper if anyone is interested: Kean Birch (2011) *Have we ever been neoliberal?* http://www.iippe.org/wiki/images/c/cd/Working_Paper_Ever_Neoliberal.pdf

13   Hodgson, G. (2005) Knowledge at work: Some neoliberal anachronisms. *Review of Social Economy* 63(4): 547-565.

14   I want to acknowledge a debt to Stephanie Mudge for the title of this section, since it is (basically) the same as one of her articles: Mudge, S. 2008. What is neo-liberalism? *Socio-Economic Review* 6:703-731.

15   In his recent book, Jamie Peck provides a useful graph of the academic popularity of the term "neoliberalism": Peck, J. (2010) *Constructions of Neoliberal Reason.* Oxford: Oxford University Press, p.13

16   See, Boas, T. and Jordan Gans-Morse, J. (2004) Neoliberalism: From New Liberal Philosophy to Anti-Liberal Slogan. *Studies in Comparative International Development* 44(2): 137-161.

17   See, for example: Birch, K. and Mykhnenko, V. (2009) Varieties of neoliberalism? Restructuring in large industrially dependent regions across Western and Eastern Europe. *Journal of Economic Geography* 9(3): 355-380; Birch, K. & Mykhnenko, V. (eds.) (2010) *The Rise and Fall of Neoliberalism: The Collapse of an Economic Order?* London: Zed Books; and, Birch, K. and Tickell, A. (2010) Making neoliberal order in the United States, in K. Birch and V. Mykhnenko (eds) *The Rise and Fall of Neoliberalism.* London:

Zed Books, pp.42-59.
18 This definition is taken from Birch, K. and Mykhnenko, V. (eds) (2010) *The Rise and Fall of Neoliberalism*. London: Zed Books, p.5.
19 It's probably worth reading Clive Barnett's critique of the concept of neoliberalism, since he takes particular issue with how it is used: Barnett, C. (2009) Publics and markets: What's wrong with neoliberalism?, in S. Smith, R. Pain, S. Marston, and J.P. Jones III (eds.) *The Sage Handbook of Social Geography*. London: Sage, pp. 269-296.
20 Foucault, M. (1979[2008]) *The Birth of Biopolitics : Lectures at the Collège de France, 1978-1979*. New York: Picador.
21 See Mirowski, P. and Plehwe, D. (eds) (2009) *The Road From Mont Pelerin*. Cambridge, MA: Harvard University Press.
22 Mudge, S. 2008. What is neo-liberalism? *Socio-Economic Review* 6: 703-731; and, Amable, B. (2011) Morals and Politics in the Ideology of Neo-liberalism. *Socio Economic Review* 9(1): 3-30.
23 Hayek, F. (1944[2001]) *The Road to Serfdom*. London: Routledge.
24 See, for example, Harvey, D. (2005) *A Brief History of Neoliberalism*. Oxford: Oxford University Press; and, Dumenil, G. and Levy, D. (2004) *Capital Resurgent: The Roots of the Neoliberal Revolution*. Cambridge, MA: Harvard University Press.
25 Peck, J. and Tickell, A. 2002. Neoliberalizing Space. *Antipode* 34 (3):380-404.

Chapter 1

Neoliberalism in Retrospect

Introduction

Having outlined the aim and structure of this book in the introductory chapter, I'm going to start the substantive chapters by looking at neoliberalism in some depth, something which, strangely enough, is rarely done by critics, with several exceptions as will become clear below. Aside from the glaring title of the book, the previous chapter should have indicated that I'm taking a critical look at neoliberalism as a concept we use all-too-freely on the left to define and describe a range of things we don't like, whether it is philosophical worldviews, government policies or political-economic change.

In this chapter, then, I'm going to delve into the dingy darkness from which neoliberalism rose and has yet to go back to. As a result, I'm probably going to go into more depth than would be usual in this sort of book; the reason I'm doing this is because I think it's important to get a good grasp of what *neoliberals* think themselves, rather than rely on second-hand criticism. Through this examination of the intellectual histories of neoliberalism – or "neoliberalisms" – I hope to highlight some of the ambiguities and contradictions that exist when we talk about neoliberal-this or neoliberal-that. Thus my purpose is to problematize the very notion that we can even identify one thing as neoliberal or neoliberal-like from the morass.

After outlining one critical take of neoliberalism drawn from the work of Michel Foucault, I then consider neoliberalism as a contested rationality – I should really hold up my hands here and admit that I've probably played fast and loose with the term in my time. Here, though, I highlight the difference between critics of neoliberalism and the supposed neoliberals themselves.

Why is there such a difference between the two? What implications does this have? My main point is that critics have allowed neoliberals to weasel out of admitting their culpability for the effects of neoliberalism because they can deny being neoliberal.

What is Neoliberalism I: Governmentality

It is probably good to start with one of the earliest writers about neoliberalism, Michel Foucault. He presented his ideas in a series of lectures at the College de France called "The Birth of Biopolitics" in 1979 – these lectures were not published in English until much later but have still proved to be highly influential.[1] In them he 'excavates' the emergence of neoliberalism, although he does so in his contemporary political context (i.e. the 1970s). According to Thomas Lemke, who has written extensively about Foucault's concept of biopolitics, what Foucault was trying to do was link the "study of the technologies of power ... [with] an analysis of the political rationality underpinning them" (p.191).[2] These two things constitute *governmentality*; the way that governments try to mould their citizens into 'productive members of society'. What this approach enables Foucault to do is explore the political rationalities behind the technologies of power that shape our behaviour and actions. What Foucault identifies is a difference between the ideas underpinning the German and the Chicago schools of neoliberalism and how these lead to different political technologies (e.g. laws, regulations, policies, etc.). For example, the former promotes state intervention to ensure market competition, while the latter promotes the downloading of state responsibilities onto individuals to force them to compete in (free) markets. Either way, what drives these changes is a rationality based on promoting market competition.

That last point is important to remember. According to Foucault,[3] neoliberalism is characterized by a distinct attitude to monopoly; neoliberals view it as "an archaic phenomenon and a phenomenon of [state] intervention" (p.135). For neoliberals like

Ludwig von Mises and Wilhelm Ropke, monopoly is particularly problematic because "it acts on prices, that is to say, on the regulatory mechanism of the economy" (p.136). What this legitimates is the introduction of "an institutional framework ... to prevent either individuals or public authorities intervening to create a monopoly" (p.137). While Foucault highlights this fear of monopoly in the Austrian and German schools of neoliberalism, he pays less attention to monopoly when it comes to what he calls American neoliberalism – basically, the 'second' Chicago school. I've outlined the differences between these various 'schools' of neoliberalism below. Why all this matters will become clearer, hopefully, when I discuss the changing attitude of neoliberals to corporate monopoly in the last third of the 20th century (see also Chapter 3).

Returning to Foucault, he sees markets as technologies of power and neoliberalism as the rationality that underpins them. In both the German and Chicago schools there is an emphasis on promoting and strengthening competitive markets in order to stop totalitarianism (or whatever else they find reprehensible); where these schools differ is in how this goal is achieved and the ways to achieve it. Thus they share the same rationality but differ in terms of the technologies that underpin it. Perhaps the most significant difference is that the German school is built on the assumption that there is a difference between society and economy, while the Chicago school – at least in its later guise – is most definitely not.[4] In fact, the second Chicago school (see Box 1.1 below) is based on a much starker and evangelical attempt to spread economic assumptions to new areas of substantive research (e.g. the law), other disciplines (e.g. sociology) and individual subjectivities (e.g. human capital theory). A recent article by Edward Nik-Khah and Robert van Horn makes this point much clearer through an historical analysis of the aims of key (second) Chicago school economists like Aaron Director and George Stigler.[5]

Obviously what I've written here is bound to have done a major disservice to the intricacies of Foucault's thought, but since many people have written whole books about it I don't feel the need, nor do I have the expertise, to do much more than sketch some interesting aspects of his analysis. I would recommend the work of Thomas Lemke, Nikolas Rose and Mitchell Dean for further reading. What I want to stress here, and you'll understand why this is important as you keep reading, is that Foucault had a rather static view of neoliberalism – he distinguished between German and American versions but didn't go into their intellectual evolution. Thinking about how neoliberal ideas (and therefore rationalities) have changed is important because we have to understand how and why attitudes to things like corporate monopoly changed over time, which can lead to contradictory positions between early and later neoliberal thinkers.

Neoliberalism as Contested Rationality

I've been writing about "neoliberalism" for several years now – again, apologies for the scare quotes but as you read it will become evident why I have put them there. Because of this, it's not easy for me to break down the concept of neoliberalism into constituent parts that are clear and unambiguous. It's difficult to recall when I first heard the term, but it was probably when I was at university in the late 1990s. It was not the most popular term at that time, for sure; others like globalization were much more in vogue, especially in the social sciences. So it wasn't until the early-2000s that I really began to engage systematically with neoliberalism as a concept beyond a mere signifier of everything bad with the world. Since then I've used the term quite frequently when writing about specific policies, processes and perspectives that have dominated our political economies since the late 1970s.

As I've mentioned already, the more I've written about neoliberalism the less sure I've become about what it actually is or means. I increasingly worry that it has become a rather fuzzy and amorphous term that can be applied to anything I look at, if only I massage the theory enough or squeeze the round peg of reality through the square hole of the analytical concept. Clearly others reject the term outright as too ideological – a term used by the left to bash anything they don't like – as well as analytically useless – see, for example, Clive Barnett's critical arguments about how neoliberalism is used.[6] In popular debates, moreover, it has become hopelessly entangled with other terms like conservative, neoconservative, libertarian, New Right, free marketer, Thatcherite, Reaganite, Washington Consensus, etc., to the extent that it is sometimes hard to tell what people are talking or writing about when they refer to 'neoliberal' or 'neoliberalism'.

One example of this entanglement is Naomi Klein's 2007 *The Shock Doctrine*.[7] Early on in the book she claims that these different perspectives (e.g. neoliberalism, conservatism, etc.) are equivalent because they "share a commitment to the policy trinity – the elimination of the public sphere, total liberation of corporations and skeletal social spending" (p.17). Although she specifically does not call this neoliberalism, preferring the term Chicago School (itself a problematic shorthand for neoliberalism), she does conflate a range of different political, theoretical and ethical perspectives and arguments. This is not to say that Klein doesn't provide some important insights in *Shock Doctrine*, far from it. She highlights the fact that while free markets are pushed as the solution to all social ills, what we tend to end up with is "the rise of corporatism" (p.18) – that is, corporate power, but unlike other forms of corporatism it's delivered on the back of violence, terror and misery (i.e. shock). I will come back to some of these issues in Chapter 2 when I talk about the rise and dominance of corporations and how this contradicts many (early) neoliberal tenets. For now, though, it is enough to highlight the frequent conflation of concepts in popular debates.

Whether or not neoliberalism is an adequate term or concept might simply be beside the point. What we are trying to define needs a term we can use to describe it, so why not use neoliberal? Funnily enough, supposed neoliberals (e.g. Milton Friedman, Alan Greenspan, etc.) don't describe themselves using these terms – in recent memory at least. For example, even though Milton Friedman wrote an essay in 1951 called "Neoliberalism and its prospects", according to Daniel Stedman Jones at least he then rarely referred to the term afterwards.[8] More importantly perhaps, Friedman changed his views considerably from those in that essay during the following decade. Moreover, in his recent book *The Great Persuasion*, Angus Burgin (pp.72-3) claims that there was significant debate about what 'neoliberals' wanted to call themselves and their program at the *Colloque Walter Lippmann* in 1938 – *the* founding event of neoliberalism which I discuss below – and "neo-liberal" was suggested but largely rejected by the participants.[9] It is interesting to note this discrepancy between self- and external identifications of neoliberals because it raises the question of whether neoliberals recognize themselves as such in the characterizations made of them by others, especially critics from the left, and whether these critical characterizations have changed so much over time that they have mutated beyond recognition and, hence, usefulness.

A History of Neoliberal Rationality

A number of scholars, who I'll come back to later in the book, have argued that there are phases or periods of neoliberalism;[10] this raises the important point that neoliberalism has evolved over time and, consequently, it is unlikely to be the same now as it was when it first emerged. Its origins are commonly traced back to the *Colloque Walter Lippmann* held in Paris in 1938. It was at this event that the term "neo-liberalism" was supposedly coined; it was meant to refer to a rejuvenated liberalism or *laissez-faire*. There are several accounts of this meeting, including pretty

Chapter 1. Neoliberalism in Retrospect

detailed ones by the likes of Francois Denord, Jamie Peck and Angus Burgin,[11] so I'm not going to repeat any of it here.

What I do want to point out, however, is that there are antecedents to this Paris meeting which are interesting in themselves. In an unpublished and undated paper, Dag Einar Thorsen and Amund Lie point out that "neo-liberalism" was a term used much earlier than the 1930s.[12] In fact what Thorsen and Lie highlight is that the Italian economist Charles Gide used the term in an 1898 article in *The Economic Journal* to refer to the work of Italian economist Maffeo Pantaleoni.[13] Here I'm going to quote a rather long passage from this article in which Gide refers to Pantaleoni and the "neo-liberal school" as promoting:

> "This hedonistic world is that in which free competition will reign absolutely; where all monopoly by right or of fact will be abolished; where every individual will be conversant with his true interests, and as well equipped as any one else to fight for them; where everything will be carried on by genuinely free contract, in which each contracting party will weigh in a subjective balance, infallibly exact, the final utility of the object to be disposed of and of the object to be acquired,-a bargaining where neither violence, nor fraud, nor lies, nor ignorance, nor dependence on others, nor any foreign disturbing element whatever-for instance the miserable preoccupation as to whether there's anything-for supper-will come in to upset so delicate an operation: a world where the law of supply and demand will bring about the maximum of utility for both individual and society, and will always send back the barometric needle, at once and without friction, to "set fair " – I mean to the fair price" (p.494-5).

Pantaleoni was an Italian economists and a strong proponent of neoclassical economics; he was also a supporter of early Italian fascism, as were other Italian economists like Luigi Einaudi who founded the Bocconi School of economics – forerunner of public choice theories – and who became governor of the Bank of Italy and then Italian president after World War 2 (WW2).[14] Both Pantaleoni and Einaudi supported the early economic policies of Benito Mussolini, who started out by promoting the return of laissez-faire through privatization as well as tax and spending cuts – later, Einaudi criticized the fascist government after it turned towards corporatism in the mid-1920s.[15] This early Italian school of neoliberal thought is important because it influenced the later work of James Buchanan from the Virginia School of neoliberalism, especially the work on public choice theory (see Figure 1.1). Unfortunately there is little information about people like Pantaleoni in English so I can only develop this discussion so far. One source I did find was Peter Groenewegen in the book *Italian Economists of the Twentieth Century* edited by Ferdinando Meacci. The picture painted of Pantaleoni by Groenewegen is very much as a supporter of free markets – and early fascism – building on utilitarian foundations (hence "hedonistic world" comment by Gide) as well as mentor and teacher of important Italian economists like Vilfred Pareto.[16] What is interesting to note is that Pantaleoni's support for early fascism shows how fascism and free markets are very much compatible; one particular example is the privatization of state-owned enterprises in Italy.[17]

At the same time as it might be possible to identify an early Italian School of neoliberal thought, it is much easier to identify the Austrian, British, German and American schools as outlines in Figure 1.1. All these schools, in some way or another, arose out of the *marginalist* revolution in economics in the late nineteenth century. For example, the Austrian school descended directly from the work of Carl Menger, while the more amorphous British school can also be traced to Menger and William Stanley Jevons through people like Lionel Robbins, as well as to the British liberal perspective through people like Edward Cannan.[18]

FIGURE 1.1: Schools of Neoliberal Thought

SCHOOL	DATES	KEY PEOPLE	KEY IDEAS
Italian	Early 20th century	Maffeo Pantaleoni, Luigi Einaudi and, to lesser extent, Vilfred Pareto	Hedonism
British	Early to mid-20th century	Edward Cannan, Lionel Robbins and, to lesser extent, Michael Polanyi	Liberalism
Austrian	Late 19th to mid-20th centuries	Ludwig von Mises, Friedrich von Hayek and their students like Fritz Machlup, Joseph Schumpeter	Subjectivism
German / Freiburg	Early to late 20th century	Walter Eucken, Wilhelm Ropke, Alexander Rustow	Ordoliberalism
1st Chicago	Early to mid-20th century	Frank Knight, Jacob Viner and Henry Simons	New liberalism
2nd Chicago	Mid-20th century to early 21st century	Milton Friedman, Aaron Director and George Stigler	(Neo-)liberalism
Virginia	Mid-20th century to early 21st century	James Buchanan	Public choice

Sources: Gide, C. (1898) Has Co-operation Introduced a New Principle into Economics? *The Economic Journal* 8: 490-511; Foucault, M. (1979[2008]) *The Birth of Biopolitics: Lectures at the Collège de France, 1978-1979*. New York: Picador; Peck, J. (2010) *Constructions of Neoliberal Reason*. Oxford: Oxford University Press; Burgin, A. (2012) *The Great Persuasion: Reinventing Free Markets since the Depression*. Cambridge, MA: Harvard University Press; Blyth, M. (2013) *Austerity*. Oxford: Oxford University Press.

These intellectual roots share a common break with classical political economy and especially the identification of objective value premised by the labour theory of value which stretched back through thinkers like Karl Marx, David Ricardo and Adam Smith. According to Alexander Shand and George Shackle, for example, subjectivists like Menger and his adherents "argued that value is not a property inherent in goods but constitutes a relationship between appraising minds and object appraised".[19] This explains why they (and later neoliberal thinkers who they influenced) placed such an emphasis on markets; from this marginalist perspective, markets provide the only mechanism to determine and coordinate all the subjective value judgements humans make.

When it comes to neoliberalism, the emergence of the Austrian school is probably the most important part of the intellectual history of neoliberal thought; without it, it would be difficult to see the other schools arising independently, although that is not to claim that the Austrian school was or is the dominant school of neoliberal thought. Two key figures in this rise and spread of the Austrian school are Ludwig von Mises (1881-1973) – an unreconstructed liberal throughout his life – and his student Friedrich von Hayek (1899-1992) – a key bridge between Europe and North America. During the 1920s both men travelled to the USA for one reason or another. In the 1930s Hayek was offered and accepted a job at the LSE in London,[20] while later in the decade von Mises ended up fleeing to New York where he lived in straightened states.[21] While in London, Hayek made connections through Lionel Robbins to the first Chicago school of Frank Knight, Jacob Viner and Henry Simons, although these Americans sometimes questioned the dogmatism of the Austrian perspective, especially von Mises.[22]

By the late 1930s there was a growing fear amongst these (economic) liberal thinkers that they were losing the intellectual war, leading to concern that countries like Britain and the United

Chapter 1. Neoliberalism in Retrospect

States would follow Germany and Russia into totalitarianism. This fear was manifested in Walter Lippman's 1937 book *The Good Society*, in which he set out, well before Hayek's 1944 *Road to Serfdom*, the argument that collective economic planning inevitably led to totalitarianism.[23] This book prompted the frequently cited foundational event of neoliberalism, the 1938 *Colloque Walter Lippmann* in Paris. This event brought together several European schools of (neo-)liberalism (e.g. British, Austrian, German) and one or two North Americans including Lippmann himself.[24] The Colloque was organized by the French philosopher Louis Rougier to discuss *The Good Society*, and was

---

Box 1.1 Manchesterism and Louis Rougier's Traffic Analogy

"To be liberal, it is not, like 'manchesterien' [i.e. nineteenth century *laissez faire*], to let cars drive in every direction, following their inclinations, which would result in difficulties and incessant accidents; it is not, like the 'planner', to determine for each car its hour of departure and its itinerary; it is to impose the *rules of the road*".

Source: Louis Rougier (1938), quoted in Angus Burgin (2012) *The Great Persuasion*. Cambridge, MA: Harvard University Press, p.72.

---

inevitably heavily attended by French liberals. In their discussion, the participants sought to 'renovate' laissez-faire for the twentieth century (see Box 1.1), junking the negative baggage of nineteenth century Manchester liberalism (e.g. social Darwinism of Herbert Spencer) and creating a positive role for the state as legal authority and enforcer of markets.[25]

Interestingly, the law comes back again and again throughout neoliberal thought and it is arguably the area where neoliberalism has had most impact, as I will try to illustrate in the next chapter with regards to monopoly and anti-trust. It is, however, rarely addressed properly in many critical accounts of neoliberalism.

Although WW2 interfered with subsequent plans for future events, it also had the unexpected side-effect of spreading these 'new' liberals and their ideas around the world as they sought to escape persecution in countries like Austria and Germany. This intellectual diaspora no doubt had a significant effect on the later influence of one School of neoliberal thought on another, especially as European perspectives moved across the Atlantic to North America and back again after the war. Another important influence was Hayek's book *The Road to Serfdom*, which was published in 1944, and his subsequent tour of the USA – this helped publicize neoliberal perspectives to a wider audience and attracted the attention of Howard Luhnow from the William Volker Fund. The work of Robert van Horn and Philip Mirowski provides a fascinating insight into how the Volker Fund was re-oriented by Luhnow towards the financing of free market ideas – I'll come back to it below.[26] The interest of Americans in Hayek's work was facilitated by his friendship with Henry Simons at the University of Chicago – an economist in the law school – which went back to the mid-1930s and the publication of Simons' *Positive Program for Laissez Faire* in 1934. It is apparent that there was ongoing dissemination between Hayek's – but not von Mises – Austrian perspective and the work of scholars in the 1st Chicago school, especially Henry Simons. This was largely financed by the Volker Fund on a number of fronts, including providing funding for University of Chicago scholars to attend the Mont Pelerin meeting in 1947.[27] This meeting is cited as the origins of much of neoliberal thinking and organization since the mid-twentieth century onwards.[28]

The 1947 meeting at Mont Pelerin brought together various

schools of neoliberal thought from across Europe and North America and led to the establishment of the still existing *Mont Pelerin Society* (MPS).[29] At this meeting the participants agreed on a *Statement of Aims* – drafted by Robbins – that outlined the threat posed by socialism and other forms of totalitarianism which had been "fostered by the growth of a view of history which denies all absolute moral standards and by the growth of theories which question the desirability of the rule of law" (see Box 1.2). The participants established a number of foundational concerns, which all schools of neoliberal thought could sign up to: first, society was under threat from socialism; second, this threat arose because private property, competitive markets and the rule of law were devalued; third, they were devalued because of moral relativism and the loss of "moral absolutes"; and, finally, that this necessitates a rethinking of the role of the state to ensure that it's retasked to support and enforce market competition and market law.

Box 1.2 Mont Pelerin Society Statement of Aims (1947)

"The group holds that these developments have been fostered by the growth of a view of history which denies all absolute moral standards and by the growth of theories which question the desirability of the rule of law. It holds further that they have been fostered by a decline of belief in private property and the competitive market; for without the diffused power and initiative associated with these institutions it is difficult to imagine a society in which freedom may be effectively preserved.

Believing that what is essentially an ideological movement must be met by intellectual argument and the reassertion of

> valid ideals, the group, having made a preliminary exploration of the ground, is of the opinion that further study is desirable inter alia in regard to the following matters:
>
> 1. The analysis and exploration of the nature of the present crisis so as to bring home to others its essential moral and economic origins.
> 2. The redefinition of the functions of the state so as to distinguish more clearly between the totalitarian and the liberal order.
> 3. Methods of re-establishing the rule of law and of assuring its development in such manner that individuals and groups are not in a position to encroach upon the freedom of others and private rights are not allowed to become a basis of predatory power.
> 4. The possibility of establishing minimum standards by means not inimical to initiative and functioning of the market.
> 5. Methods of combating the misuse of history for the furtherance of creeds hostile to liberty.
> 6. The problem of the creation of an international order conducive to the safeguarding of peace and liberty and permitting the establishment of harmonious international economic relations."
>
> **Source:** Mont Pelerin Society website, https://www.montpelerin.org/montpelerin/mpsGoals.html

While the MPS has obviously been an influential intellectual seedbed for neoliberal ideas, it only partly shows that there was any coherence to the neoliberal schools of thought at their origins. Several subsequent historical events, accidents, etc. show

how diverse these schools of neoliberalism actually were:

(a) For one, the German school's "state-first" perspective (outlined above) was specifically concerned with promoting market competition through the state not despite it (cf. Chicago school), and was implemented as part of the political-economic transformation of Germany after WW2. These "ordoliberals", as the German school became known, were central players in the reformation of the German state and establishment of the *social market economy* after 1948 – the social market economy is now strongly associated with social democracy. For example, Ludwig Erhard, first Minister of Economic Affairs and then Chancellor, was an adherent to Wilhelm Ropke's ideas which he enacted through the wholesale elimination of Nazi-era wage and price controls. What is interesting, in light of other incidences I mention, is that these ordoliberals comprised more than one lawyer.[30]

(b) For another, the Austrian school essentially disintegrated as Hayek and von Mises went their own ways. Even though their ideas were no doubt influential, they no longer constituted a clear school of neoliberal thought. In 1950 Hayek, for example, moved to the University of Chicago, although his appointment was in the Committee on Social Thought and not Economics. This was financed by the Volker Fund and would seemingly tie Hayek into the evolving Chicago school. However, his work veered off in other directions as the second Chicago school took shape during the 1950s and 1960s.[31]

(c) Finally, the British school, which was the most diffuse anyway, gradually eroded as the likes of Hayek left and others, like Robbins, moved to more mainstream (i.e. Keynesian) positions or, like Michael Polanyi, into other areas. It is perhaps surprising that British (neo-)liberals ended up shunted into thinks tanks like the IEA or isolated in Economic departments, but it might also help to explain their re-emergence later with the rise of Thatcher as they were less tied to orthodoxies in university departments.[32]

What is obvious is that the centre of neo-liberal thought had shifted over the Atlantic, especially to the University of Chicago where people like Milton Friedman, George Stigler and Aaron Director took over not only from the first Chicago school but also from the Austrian and other schools as the dominant free market thinkers. Their distinctive approach is well documented in a number of books including ones already mentioned. There are others like Johan van Overtveltd's *The Chicago School* and van Horn, Mirowski and Stapleford's edited collection, *Building Chicago Economics*.[33] The former author clearly identifies two Chicago schools, the second emerging in the late 1950s and comprising scholars in the Economics department and Law school. What differentiates the first and second school most is the differing attitudes to corporate monopoly, an issue I discuss next.

Evolution of Neoliberal Rationality regarding Corporate Monopoly

One area of research on the intellectual histories of neoliberalism that has proved particularly insightful of late is the work on neoliberal attitudes to monopoly, especially corporate or business monopoly. Considering the silence (at best) and even support (at worst) of free market advocates for corporate power and monopoly, it seems strange to think that neoliberals – even in the second Chicago school – were vociferous opponents of monopoly, in all its forms, not that long ago. In fact, this antipathy to monopoly is what differentiated neoliberalism from laissez-faire (i.e. old liberalism) in the first place. It is the reason, for example, why neoliberal thinkers argued that there needed to be a 'positive' (i.e. active) role for the state, as opposed to its simple erosion or hollowing-out. A strong state was deemed necessary because it would help to create, maintain and enforce competitive markets which had descended into monopolistic cartels at the end of the nineteenth century.

According to early neoliberal thinkers 'free' markets are human constructions, they are not naturally occurring – this obviously contrasts with both nineteenth century and contemporary rhetoric about self-regulating markets. The former, of more relevance here, arises from the shift from classical political economy to neoclassical economics with the marginalist revolution after 1870, which reoriented the foundations of economic theory from production to market exchange based on assumptions of individual rationality and perfect competition.[34] These assumptions predicted that the most efficient distribution of resources in society was through free markets – anything less was, therefore, detrimental to society and should be avoided or intentionally removed. However, as Karl Polanyi outlined in *The Great Transformation*,[35] this laissez faire perspective was premised on a night-watchman state and limited intervention in markets, primarily to stop the resulting concentration of economic power in fewer and fewer hands as became evident in the 'Robber Barons' era in the USA at the end of the nineteenth century.

Here is where neo-liberalism comes in as an alternative to laissez-faire. Not only does it offer a solution to the problem of monopoly and economic power, it also promises to resolve this issue while promoting free markets and ending the slide to socialism and fascism – it's perhaps worth noting that socialism is the most feared of these two totalitarian regimes.[36] The purpose of a strong state is to stop business monopoly and concentrations of economic power, as much as it is to stop the power of labour. For example, in his 1934 *Positive Program for Laissez Faire*, Henry Simons argued that: *"the great enemy of democracy is monopoly, in all its forms*: gigantic corporations, trade associations and other agencies for price control, trade unions".[37] This is a perspective Simons repeats in work published in 1948, after his death: "There must be vigorous and vigilant prosecution of conspiracy in restraint of trade and, above all, thoroughgoing reform of corporate law".[38]

In rethinking liberalism, people like Simons sought to promote a 'free economy' through a strong state, effectively endorsing some form of state regulation, and even redistribution. With the exception of Ludwig von Mises, other leading neoliberal thinkers of the time agreed with these ideas, supporting the notion that the state creates the institutions necessary for 'competitive order' and markets to function. Early neoliberalism was not, thus, set against state intervention; rather, it very much endorsed said intervention as long as it was directed at creating and maintaining markets. It is therefore not unusual to find that during the 1920s, 1930s, 1940s and 1950s most neoliberal thinkers from across the various schools of neoliberal thought agreed with Simons. For example, the likes of Wilhelm Ropke, Alexander Rustow, Jacob Viner, Lionel Robbins, Milton Friedman and Friedrich von Hayek all argued for the curtailment of business monopolies (see Box 1.3)

Box 1.3 Neoliberal Perspective on Monopoly in 1920s-50s

- **Wilhelm Ropke** (1923) - liberals should fight "for the idea of the state and against the lack of freedom in which private economic monopolies – supported by government leading a shadow existence – keep the economy captive" (quoted in Turner 2008: 82).

- **Jacob Viner** (1931) - "Nothing in the history of

American business justified undue confidence on the part of the American public that it can trust big business to take care of the community without supervision, regulation or eternal vigilance" (quoted in Burgin 2012: 37-8).

Alexander Rustow (1932) - "his advocacy of a strong state that would protect the market economy while suppressing cartels" (Burgin 2012: 74).

Henry Simons (1934) - *"the great enemy of democracy is monopoly, in all its* forms: gigantic corporations, trade associations and other agencies for price control, trade unions" (quoted in Jackson 2010: 142).

Lionel Robbins (1934) - "The cartelisation of industry, the growth of the strength of trade unions, the multiplication of State controls, have created an economic structure which, whatever its ethical or aesthetic superiority, is certainly much less capable of rapid adaption than was the older more competitive system" (quoted in Burgin 2012: 26).

Friedrich von Hayek (1944) - "This conclusion is strongly supported by the historical order in which the decline of competition and the growth of monopoly manifested themselves in different countries" (p.52); "the impetus of the movement toward totalitarianism comes mainly from the two great vested interests: organized capital and organized labor" (p.213) (quotes from *The Road to Serfdom*, 1944).

Henry Simons (1948) - "There must be vigorous and vigilant prosecution of conspiracy in restraint of trade and, above all, thoroughgoing reform of corporate law" (quoted in van Horn and Mirowski 2009).

Milton Friedman (1951) - "it [laissez faire] underestimated the danger that private individuals could through agreement and combination usurp power and effectively limit the freedom of other individuals" (quoted in Burgin 2012: 170).

George Stigler (1952) - "[Stigler] had gone so far as to recommend the "dissolution" of all companies that demonstrate "monopoly power"" (Burgin 2012: 172).

Sources: Hayek, F. (1944[2001]) *The Road to Serfdom*. London: Routledge; Turner, R. (2008) *Neo-Liberal Ideology*. Edinburgh: Edinburgh University Press; van Horn, R. (2009) Reinventing Monopoly and Corporations: The Roots of Chicago Law and Economics, in P. Mirowski and D. Plehwe (eds) *The Road from Mont Pelerin*. Cambridge, MA: Harvard University Press; van Horn, R. and Mirowski, P. (2009) The Rise of the Chicago School of Economics, in P. Mirowski and D. Plehwe (eds) *The Road from Mont Pelerin*. Cambridge, MA: Harvard University Press; Jackson, B. (2010) At the Origins of Neo-Liberalism: The Free Economy and the Strong State 1930-47. *Historical Journal* 53(1): 129-151; Peck, J. (2010) *Constructions of Neoliberal Reason*. Oxford: Oxford University Press; Burgin, A. (2012) *The Great Persuasion: Reinventing Free Markets since the Depression*. Cambridge, MA: Harvard University Press.

Although some neoliberals espoused anti-monopoly views into the 1970s,[39] what is evident is that view of corporate monopoly – not government monopoly – underwent a significant transformation in the 1950s and 1960s; it actually reversed and can help us to differentiate between the first and second Chicago schools. What is clear, however, is that before the mid to late 1950s even people like Milton Friedman, Aaron Director and George Stigler – the three key players in the second Chicago school – held negative views of business monopoly.[40] For example, Friedman argued that in 1952 that: "The state will police the system, it will establish the conditions favorable to competition and prevent monopoly".[41] He repeated this position a decade later in his 1962 book *Capitalism and Freedom*: e.g. "The first and most urgent necessity in the area of government policy is the elimination of those measures which directly support monopoly, whether enterprise monopoly or labor monopoly ... Both should be subjected to the anti-trust laws".[42]

As mentioned, the change in attitude distinguishes the first from the second Chicago school. From the 1950s people like Friedman, Director and Stigler shifted their perspectives significantly, essentially reversing their initial opinions on corporate monopoly. Much of the research highlighting this change has been done by Robert van Horn, Edward Nik-Khah and their collaborators like Philip Mirowski, and is really worth reading for detailed accounts of what lay behind this change.[43] All I can really do here is give a brief synopsis. Basically, this shift towards monopoly resulted from two research projects called the *Free Market Study* (1946-1952) and the *Anti-Trust Project* (1953-1957) carried out at the University of Chicago and funded by the Volker Fund. The conclusions of these projects were that the threat of monopoly in the 1930s and 1940s "had been substantially overestimated".[44] These findings led to this shift in the perspective of Chicago school economists towards public regulation, which they came to view as more "dangerous" than corporate monopoly. Subsequent decades were witness to an increasing interest by Chicago school thinkers in the study and critique of anti-trust regulation (designed to stop corporate monopolies developing); what basically happened is that these Chicagoans ended up becoming very comfortable with the concentration of economic power in the hands of large corporations. During the 1960s and 1970s the concern with corporate monopoly evolved into an outright attack on government sanctioned monopolies and anti-trust regulations, rather than any distorting effects of private monopoly power. As Will Davies illustrates in his article in *Economy and Society*, this translated into influence over US competition policy during the 1970s and 1980s. So, even though Chicagoans like "Stigler continued to advocate a policy of industrial de-concentration through the 1950s and 1960s, and most leading Chicago economists followed suit", others at Chicago such as Aaron Director took on anti-trust regulation from the 1950s onwards.[45] In their conversion, Davies points out that these Chicagoans used transaction cost economics to justify corporate monopolies (discussed in Chapter 3); e.g. large corporations, benefiting from the efficiencies of hierarchical organization, could provide consumers with cheaper goods than 'free' market transactions. Hence monopolies could be more efficient than markets and therefore justifiable.

Now, van Horn and Mirowski argue that is was from the 1950s that the second Chicago School took up the task of supporting corporate monopolies, in contrast to the earlier concern in the 1930s and 1940s with the concentration of ownership and power. It is a good example of how these thinkers adapted their ideas to the context in which they found themselves (e.g. the power of large corporations), rather than seeking to adapt their context to their perspective as is often argued. As the ideas of Chicagoans shifted in the latter half of the twentieth century, the evolution of their thought turned early neoliberal thinking on its head. They provided theoretical support for the concentration of capital in large corporations, legitimating large corporations as efficient market actors providing consumer benefits through falling prices – this contrasted with earlier claims about corporate monopolies distorting the proper functioning of markets. Funnily enough, the best way neoliberals could support this corporate expansion was – as earlier neoliberals themselves pointed out disapprovingly – to support government intervention in the economy. Not just limited intervention either, but large-scale intervention, whether in the form of regulatory interventions or financial underwriting. Without such government intervention monopoly would be eroded.

Conclusion

What does all this mean? How does it relate to the central concern of this book? Well, if we accept the idea of neoliberalism as governmentality, posited by Foucault and others (see above), what I've outlined in this chapter raises some tricky questions. Namely, at what point in history do the specifically neoliberal technologies of power and accompanying rationalities kick in, as it were? This is difficult to answer if we acknowledge the diversity of neoliberal thinking and evolution of neoliberal positions on major topics like corporate monopoly. Do the technologies start before rationalities, for example? This would imply that technologies of power like anti-trust regulation accompany anti-monopoly perspectives, which they did but well before so-called neoliberals were on the scene (e.g. 1890s and early 1900s). Does that mean that anti-trust and anti-monopoly ideas are not neoliberal? Hardly; they dominated much of neoliberal thinking in the first half of the twentieth century. What it might suggest is that anti-trust regulation was a neoliberal technology (even though it arose in the late nineteenth century), but then stopped being one when the neoliberal rationality changed as the second Chicago school reversed its perspective in the 1950s and 1960s.

This raises further issues with the governmentality. It's necessary to think about how change happens and what this means to various governance technologies and rationalities. Do technologies of power and rationalities, for example, change at the same time? Which changes first? Which drives change? Do technologies shape rationalities, or vice versa? What the discussion of corporate monopoly should hopefully illustrate is that neoliberal rationalities have changed in response to forces (or technologies, if you like) that are not necessarily neoliberal. So, neoliberals of the second Chicago mold became very comfortable using their scholarship to support and even promote large corporations. Large corporations have been around for some time, stretching back to the nineteenth century,[46] which suggests that they cannot be a specifically neoliberal 'technology'.

What this chapter should have shown is that there has been a slew of recent scholarship on the intellectual histories of neoliberalism which problematizes the neat separation and relation between neoliberal rationalities and technologies. I would strongly recommend reading this literature for the insight it provides into the evolution of the different schools of neoliberal thought and how this has impacted (or not) on the transformation of our societies. Just a few examples include Angus Burgin's *The Great Persuasion*, Daniel Stedman Jones' *Masters of the Universe*, and Jamie Peck's *Construction of Neoliberal Reason*. A lot of other research by the likes of Philip Mirowski, Robert van Horn, Edward Nik-Khan, Ben Jackson and so on is also really worth looking at. I don't want to criticize this research, since it has been very important, but I want to suggest that because of its focus on the intellectual evolution of neoliberalism it only provides one side of the story – that is, it only provides an insight into the ideas behind the rise of neoliberalism and not the social, political and economic forces that have influenced the evolution of neoliberal positions. I'm basically arguing that neoliberalism has been shaped by these forces, rather than that these forces have been shaped by neoliberalism.

Overall then, it has been my intention in this chapter to provide a short, yet hopefully interesting, history of the intellectual development and diversity of neoliberalism – as we know it. My reason for doing so is to show that we cannot identify any single or homogenous 'neoliberal' rationality or immutable and static neoliberal technologies. It is in this sense that I claim we have never been neoliberal – it is always evolving, becoming something new, something different. Thus we can't actually be neoliberal because we can't identify a neoliberal rationality as opposed to neoliberal rationalities – there are too many choices, too many changes, too many variations on a theme to make any sensible claim otherwise. For example, what we now think of as social democracy in Germany started out as a neoliberal school of thought, ordoliberalism. Moreover, by the 1960s the Chicago school had mutated beyond the recognition of those in the first Chicago school, and has probably changed once again since then. One key area where these differences are most glaring is the attitudes of these different schools of neoliberalism to corporate monopoly. It is this issue that represents a key break between more recent versions of neoliberalism – e.g. second Chicago school – and most of the earlier schools. I come back to this issue in later chapters to consider what led to the concentration of economic power and what this has meant for understanding neoliberalism in the UK, USA and Canada.

1   Foucault, M. (1979[2008]) *The Birth of Biopolitics: Lectures at the Collège de France, 1978-1979*. New York: Picador.
2   Lemke, T. (2001) The birth of bio-politics: Michael Foucault's lectures at the College de France on neo-liberal governmentality. *Economy and Society* 30(2): 190-207.
3   Foucault, *The Birth of Biopolitics*, note 1.
4   This point is made by Francesco Guala in his review of

Foucault's arguments: Guala, F. (2006) Review of Michel Foucault, *Naissance de la biopolitique: Cours au Collège de France, 1978-1979*. *Economics and Philosophy* 22, 429-439.

5   Nik-Khah, E. and van Horn, R. (2012) Inland Empire: Economics Imperialism as an Imperative of Chicago Neoliberalism. *Journal of Economic Methodology* 19(3): 259-282.

6   Barnett, C. (2009) Publics and markets: What's wrong with neoliberalism?, in S. Smith, R. Pain, S. Marston, and J.P. Jones III (eds.) *The Sage Handbook of Social Geography*. London: Sage, pp. 269-296.

7   Klein, N. (2007) *Shock Doctrine*. Toronto: Vintage Canada.

8   Jones, D.S. (2012) *Masters of the Universe: Hayek, Friedman, and the Birth of Neoliberal Politics*. Connecticut: Princeton University Press.

9   Burgin, A. (2012) *The Great Persuasion: Reinventing Free Markets since the Depression*. Cambridge, MA: Harvard University Press.

10 See, for example, Tickell, A. and Peck, J. (2003) Making global rules: globalization or neoliberalization?, in J. Peck and H. Yeung (eds) *Remaking the Global Economy*. London: Sage, pp.163-181.

11 See, Denord, F. (2009) French neo-liberalism and its divisions: From the Colloque Walter Lippmann to the 5th Republic, in P. Mirowski and D. Plehwe (eds) *The Road from Mont-Pèlerin: The making of the neoliberal thought collective*. Cambridge, MA: Harvard University Press, pp.45-67; Peck, J. (2010) *Constructions of Neoliberal Reason*. Oxford: Oxford University Press; and, Burgin, *The Great Persuasion*, note ix.

12 Thorsen, D.E. and Lie, A. (undated) What is Neoliberalism? Available online: http://folk.uio.no/daget/What%20is%20Neo-Liberalism%20FINAL.pdf

13 Gide, C. (1898) Has Co-operation Introduced a New Principle into Economics? *The Economic Journal* 8:490-511.

14 Blyth, M. (2013) *Austerity*. Oxford: Oxford University Press, pp.165-6.
15 Faucci, R. (2004) From corporative 'Programmed Economy' to Post-War planning: Some notes on the debate among Italian economists, in R. Arena and N. Salvadori (eds) *Money, Credit and the Role of the State*. Aldershot: Ashgate, p.416.
16 Gorenewegen, P. (1998) Maffeo Pantaleoni, in F. Meacci (ed.) *Italian Economists of the 20th Century*. Cheltenham: Edward Elgar.
17 Bel, G. (2011) The first privatization: Selling SOEs and privatizing public monopolies in fascist Italy (1922-1925). *Cambridge Journal of Economics* 35(5): 937-956.
18 Shand, A. and Shackle, G. (1980) *Subjectivist Economics*. Exeter: Pica Press; Cockett, R. (1995) *Thinking the Unthinkable: Think-tanks and the Economic Counter-revolution, 1931-1983*. London: Harper Collins Publishers; and, Burgin, *The Great Persuasion*, note ix.
19 Shand and Shackle, *Subjectivist Economics*, note 18, p.13.
20 At the LSE, Hayek influenced the likes of Ronald Coase who I'll come back to in the next chapter.
21 Birch, K. and Mykhnenko, V. (eds) (2010) *The Rise and Fall of Neoliberalism*. London: Zed Books
22 Burgin, *The Great Persuasion*, note 9.
23 Ibid.
24 Participants included a number of people from across French society, as well as British-based academics and members of the Austrian and German schools of neoliberalism; see, Denord, 'French neo-liberalism and its divisions', note 11. A more accessible list of people is available on the French Wikipedia website: http://fr.wikipedia.org/wiki/Colloque_Walter_Lippmann
25 Cockett, *Thinking the Unthinkable*, note 18, pp. 9-12.
26 Van Horn, R. and Mirowski, P. (2009) The Rise of the

Chicago School of Economics, in by P. Mirowski and D. Plehwe (eds) *The Road from Mont Pelerin*. Harvard: Harvard University Press.

27 This includes Milton Friedman, George Stigler, Aaron Director and Frank Knight, but not Henry Simons who had died the year earlier, possibly as a result of suicide; see, van Horn and Mirowski, 'The Rise of the Chicago School of Economics', note 26; and also, Caldwell, B. (2011) The Chicago School, Hayek, and Neoliberalism, in R. van Horn, P. Mirowski and T. Stapleford (eds) *Building Chicago Economics*. Cambridge: Cambridge University Press.

28 See P. Mirowski and D. Plehwe (eds) (2009) *The Road from Mont Pelerin*. Harvard: Harvard University Press.

29 Mont Pelerin Society website: https://www.montpelerin.org/montpelerin/index.html

30 See, Lemke, 'The birth of bio-politics', note 2; Peck, *Constructions of Neoliberal Reason*, note 11; Burgin, *The Great Persuasion*, note 9; and, Peck, J. (2008) Remaking laissez-faire. *Progress in Human Geography* 32: 3-43.

31 Peck, *Constructions of Neoliberal Reason*, note 11; and, Burgin, *The Great Persuasion*, note 9.

32 Cockett, *Thinking the* Unthinkable, note 18.

33 Van Overtveldt, J. (2007) *The Chicago School: How the University of Chicago Assembled the Thinkers Who Revolutionized Economics and Business*. Agate Publishing; and, van Horn, R., Mirowski, P. and Stapleford, T. (eds) (2011) *Building Chicago Economics*. Cambridge: Cambridge University Press.

34 See John F. Henry's work in this area, including Henry, J. (2008) The Ideology of the Laissez Faire Program. *Journal of Economic Issues* 42: 209-224; and, Henry, J. (2010) The historic roots of the neoliberal program. *Journal of Economic Issues* 44(2): 543-550. It's probably also worthwhile reading Fine, B. (2010) Zombieconomics: The Living Death of the Dismal

Science in the Age of Neo-Liberalism, in K.Birch and V.Mykhnenko (eds) *The Rise and Fall of Neoliberalism*. London: Zed Books.
35   Polanyi, K. (1944[2001]) *The Great Transformation*. Boston: Beacon Press.
36   There has been a recent debate sparked by a recent article by Corey Robin in which he spells out the direct links between neoliberal thinkers like Friedman and Hayek and totalitarian regimes like the Pinochet dictatorship in Chile; see Robin, C. (2013) Nietzsche's Marginal Children: On Friedrich Hayek. *The Nation* (27 May), available online: http://www.thenation.com/article/174219/nietzsches-marginal-children-friedrich-hayek#axzz2Z8oBQeqB. There is also a follow-up piece that's worth reading, available online: http://coreyrobin.com/2013/06/25/the-hayek-pinochet-connection-a-second-reply-to-my-critics/
37   Quoted in this excellent article, Jackson, B. (2010) At the Origins of Neo-Liberalism: The Free Economy and the Strong State 1930-47. *Historical Journal* 53(1): 129-151.
38   Quoted in van Horn and Mirowski, 'The Rise of the Chicago School of Economics', note 26.
39   Examples include Hayek (e.g. "It is also necessary that their [laws] positive content be such as to make the market mechanism operate satisfactorily. This requires in particular rules which favor the preservation of competition and restrain, so far as possible, the development of monopolistic positions") and Murray Rothbard (e.g. "the real antipode to liberty today is the existing Corporate Monopoly Welfare-Warfare State ... it is precisely Big Business that is largely responsible for the twentieth century march into aggressive statism"), who both espoused these such anti-monopoly views in 1973. Both quotes come from Caldwell, 'The Chicago School Hayek, and Neoliberalism', note 27.
40   A range of material is relevant here, including work by

Edward Nik-Khah: e.g. Nik-Khah, E. (2011) George Stigler, the Graduate School of Business, and the Pillars of the Chicago School, in R. van Horn, P. Mirowski, and T. Stapleford (eds) *Building Chicago Economics: New Perspectives on the History of America's Most Powerful Economics Program*. New York: Cambridge University Press, pp. 116-147; and, Nik-Khah, E. and van Horn, R. (2012) Inland Empire: Economics Imperialism as an Imperative of Chicago Neoliberalism. *Journal of Economic Methodology* 19(3): 259-282. People like Robert van Horn have also dealt with this issue: e.g. van Horn, R. (2009) Reinventing Monopoly and Corporations: The Roots of Chicago Law and Economics, in P. Mirowski and D. Plehwe (eds) *The Road from Mont Pelerin*. Cambridge, MA: Harvard University Press; and, van Horn, R. (2011) Chicago's Shifting Position on Concentrations of Business Power. *Seattle University Law Review* 34(4): 1527-1544. Finally, there's also work I've already mentioned, including: van Horn and Mirowski, 'The Rise of the Chicago School of Economics', note 26.

41 Quoted in Peck, *Constructions of Neoliberal Reason*, note 11.
42 Friedman, M. (1962[2002]) *Capitalism and Freedom*. Chicago: University of Chicago Press.
43 Van Horn, 'Reinventing Monopoly and Corporations', note 40; van Horn and Mirowski, 'The Rise of the Chicago School of Economics', note 26; and, Nik-Khah, 'George Stigler, the Graduate School of Business, and the Pillars of the Chicago School', note 40.
44 Caldwell, 'The Chicago School, Hayek, and Neoliberalism', note 27.
45 Davies, W. (2010) Economics and the 'nonsense' of law: The case of the Chicago antitrust revolution. *Economy and Society* 39(1), pp.71-2
46 Prechel, H. (2000) *Big Business and the State*. Albany: State University of New York Press.

Chapter 2

Monetarism and Fiscal Prudence vs. Ballooning Public Debt

Introduction

The previous chapter highlighted the importance of thinking about the intellectual history of neoliberalism; this chapter is about the influence of the actual ideas – intellectual and moral – that neoliberals come up with. Have they influenced policy-making? What impact have they had? How has this influence happened? That sort of thing. The reason it is important to ask these sorts of questions is that a number of critics of neoliberalism have argued that ideas are influential, so it is not just material interests (e.g. wealth and income changes) that matter in our understanding of why neoliberalism has emerged as the dominant rationality of the last 30-40 years. In this sense, I'm trying to build on what I discussed in the last chapter by looking at the specific 'neoliberal' ideas (or *rationalities* if we want to use Foucault's term) underpinning specific 'neoliberal' policies (or *technologies of power*).

As mentioned in the introduction, one of the key ways that critics define neoliberalism is by referring to monetarism; this includes the theoretical ideas supporting monetary policies (see Box 2.1 below) designed to maintain low inflation by controlling a country's money supply – don't worry, I'll come back to this and explain what this all means. Monetarism, in turn, is constituted by tight public spending and public spending cuts – that is, austerity. Since the global financial crisis (GFC), austerity has become the dominant policy paradigm – see Mark Blyth's new book *Austerity: A History of a Dangerous Idea* for more on this.[1] Both these ideas, monetarism and tight public spending, are related to one another in neoliberal arguments, forming a key idea that has supposedly informed policy-making since the 1970s – which is something I'll come back to below. As specific neoliberal ideas, they are both worth considering in some depth in order to understand whether they have impacted on government policies and, if so, how this impact has manifested itself. The latter point is also important because an idea can still be influential even if it doesn't lead to changes spelled out in that idea.

Briefly, what I do in this chapter is take issue with the way some critics have characterized neoliberalism as a set of powerful ideas – specifically, the argument that ideas promoting monetarism and tight public spending have constituted particular policies we could identify as neoliberal. As before, I'm not the first person to make this sort of point as the work of Monica Prasad in *The Politics of Free Markets* illustrates.[2] Critics frequently and loosely describe neoliberalism as comprising monetarism, referring in particular to the co-called 1979 *Volcker Shock* (see Box 2.3 below) as the prime example of this claim. What is missed, however, from these accounts is the extent to which ideas like monetarism and tight public spending actually failed (and continue to fail) to impact policy-making in the Atlantic Heartland – in fact, it is possible to illustrate that neither idea (or rationality in the Foucauldian sense) had more than a brief direct impact and that much of the influence of these ideas has been ideological or moral (legitimating policy-making), rather than political-economic (underpinning actual policies). For example, even at the end of his life in 2004, and during the Bush Jnr. presidency, Milton Friedman argued that:

"After World War II, opinion was socialist while practice was free market; currently, opinion is free market while practice is heavily socialist. We have largely won the battle of ideas (though no such battle is even won permanently); we have succeeded in stalling the progress of socialism, but we have not succeeded in reversing its course. We are still far from bringing practice into conformity with opinion."[3]

To start this chapter then, I'll outline another critical take on neoliberalism which stresses the strength of neoliberal ideas in the rise of neoliberalism in the Atlantic Heartland; this draws on a range of critical scholarship. After that I'll specifically focus on monetarism as a 'failed' idea, one that was not successfully translated into policy even though it has been very influential. I'll then turn to tight public spending as another example of a failed idea. Using both these examples I'll finish by discussing what sorts of actual policies resulted from these ideas; specifically, a massive expansion of the national public debt in countries like the USA, UK and, to a lesser extent, Canada.

What is Neoliberalism II: Ideas to Shape the World?

The critical perspective of neoliberalism I'm considering in this chapter place a particular emphasis on the power of ideas, identifying (neoliberal) ideological, philosophical and/or moral views as particularly influential in shaping the world. One misunderstanding I want to clear up now is that neoliberalism equates to (neoclassical) economics; this is not the case. In fact, I'll argue later in the book that neoliberalism – if that's what we want to call it – is derived as much from the work of scholars in business and law schools as economic departments – see Chapter 3. Here, however, I'm more concerned with the ideas that constitute neoliberal rationality, to keep using Foucault's term. Like the other perspectives on neoliberalism, there are numerous accounts of it as an ideology, set of ideas, thought collective, moral program, and so on. All I can do here then is cover some of the ground and leave the rest for the reader to uncover themselves.

A good starting point is the work of Mark Blyth, professor at Brown University, and his book *Great Transformations*.[4] In this book, Blyth is very specifically concerned with how ideas influence societal change. He identifies a confluence of ideas and theories comprising monetarism, rational expectations, supply-side economics and public choice as "disembedding liberalism" (Ch.5) – the dominant political-economic regime in the US, UK and Canada after WW2 – and leading to the emergence of neoliberalism. These ideas helped to reorient policy-making by focusing attention on specific issues (e.g. inflation), the problems associated with these issues and the threat they posed to different political constituencies (e.g. investors) – I'll come back to some of this in Chapters 4 and 5.

For now it is helpful to highlight that Blyth largely focuses on ideas drawn from the discipline of economics and doesn't really explore other philosophical, ideological or moral underpinnings of 'neoliberalism'. These are, however, taken up by other scholars. This is important to consider because many neoliberals had direct experience with totalitarianism, having been driven out of their home countries because of their beliefs, and were driven by their moral and ideological ideas as much as economic ones. Accordingly, these ideological-philosophical and moral ideas are as important an underlying motivation for neoliberals as any economic argument.[5] The sociologist Stephanie Mudge, for example, argues that neoliberalism is as much a 'moral project', as economic one, in which markets are a presented as a prerequisite for freedom.[6] To achieve freedom, however, necessitates a moral attack on alternatives, as Pierre Bourdieu outlined in the French newspaper *Le Monde Diplomatique*:

> "It [neoliberalism] adds its own symbolic force to these relations of force. In the name of a scientific programme, converted into a plan of political action, an immense *political project* is underway... This project aims to create the conditions under which the "theory" can be realised and can function: *a programme of the methodical destruction of collectives.*"[7]

Chapter 2. Monetarism and Fiscal Prudence vs. Ballooning Public Debt

The ideological antipathy to collective planning and action may arise from a set of theoretical arguments, but it has been pursued as a moral and political project to denounce collective action, especially socialism, as a threat to capitalism and as a greater threat than capitalism could ever be. This is evident in Walter Lippman's 1937 book *The Good Society* as well as later work by Hayek (e.g. *Road to Serfdom*, 1944) and Friedman (e.g. *Capitalism as Freedom*, 1962); it is also visible in the foundational statement of the Mont Pelerin Society which stressed "absolute moral standards".[8] The moral and ideological side of neoliberalism helps to explain how the economic side ends up enrolled in quite diverse – and sometimes directly contradictory – political campaigns and manifestos. This is the case especially when it comes to conservative political parties, something I've written about with Adam Tickell.[9] Others like Philip Mirowski and his co-authors have argued that neoliberalism is a "thought collective",[10] by which they mean it is a community of similarly-minded thinkers and doers who reinforce each other's points of view.[11] This thought collective was centred on the Mont Pelerin Society (MPS) – mentioned in the last chapter – and other sites of intellectual propagation, exchange and dissemination, including a range of free market and/or conservative think tanks like the Institute of Economic Affairs (UK – est. 1955), Heritage Foundation (USA – est. 1973) and Fraser Institute (Canada – est. 1974).

Again, what I've outlined here is a crude caricature of these many thinkers' ideas – I can't do much more than touch on a few strands of their arguments, unfortunately. What it has hopefully shown is that both economic and moral ideas are central to any understanding of neoliberalism, although there is a distinct contradiction between the two that commonly afflicts neoliberal/conservative positions (e.g. capitalism degrading morality) – whether these contradictory impulses are compatible is doubtful and implies that the direct influence of neoliberal ideas on policy (via political parties) is likely to be messy, to say the least. I'd recommend the work of Philip Mirowski, Mark Blyth, and Stephanie Mudge for further reading if the reader so desires. It might also be interesting to read Monica Prasad's book *The Politics of Free Markets*. What is important to note, for now, is that the former scholars are largely presenting an argument emphasizing the powerful role of ideas in creating political-economic change, a perspective which I'm going to interrogate in the rest of the chapter.

Monetarism and Tight Public Spending: 'Thinking Like a Neoliberal'

To begin with, it is important to note that neoliberals – for want of a better word – like Friedrich Hayek and Milton Friedman based much of their theoretical work on the argument that price stability is critical for the proper functioning of markets. Basically what this means is that markets can't work if people don't know what prices will be in a week's, month's or year's time – therefore, it's important to control inflation in order to ensure that prices remain stable (which doesn't mean they can't rise). What this meant – and still means – was that neoliberals tended to focus on monetary policy – that is, the control of the money supply and inflation (see Box 2.1) – as the key site of theoretical engagement with other political-economic perspectives like Keynesianism. It is also seen as the key site of government or policy intervention, one that is positive because it ensures the 'proper' functioning of markets. My argument here will require the reader to do two things over the next few pages. First, put aside any political preferences, especially any anti-neoliberal views, in order to think like a neoliberal – obviously a difficult thing to do, but one that is helpful if we want to understand where they are coming from. Second, to learn some monetary theory – which I'll try to do gently for those not familiar with it – and its relationship to public spending.

> **Box 2.1 Monetary Policy and Fiscal Policy**
>
> Both fiscal and monetary policy can be used to influence the economy. They are both about influencing 'macroeconomic' variables like savings, investment, unemployment, prices and inequality. Fiscal policy basically concerns taxation and government spending; these can be raised or lowered as needed to stimulate a declining economy (expansionary policy) or dampen a booming one (contractionary policy). Monetary policy refers to the management of the money supply and inflation in an economy; nowadays this is done through interest rate movements. According to monetarists like Milton Friedman, raising the money supply creates inflation as more money is chasing the same amount of goods leading to price rises. This can be beneficial in a recession (expansionary policy), but can erode the value of assets if inflation rises too fast.
>
> **Source:** Michael Barrett Brown (1984) *Models in Political Economy*. London: Penguin.

Think Like a Neoliberal
Generally, we could argue that a concern with monetary policy is the foundation on which much supposedly neoliberal thinking has rested. It has also had a strong influence on the policy-making decisions of supposedly neoliberal governments. Many things that are now identified as neoliberal – e.g. privatization of national industries and public utilities, liberalization of trade and capital movement, deregulation, etc. – have one thing in common; they are premised on a particular understanding of the economy in which the stability of money and the dangers of

inflation are key concerns. Hence, understanding monetarist ideas is central to understanding neoliberal policies – if we accept that these other things (e.g. privatization, deregulation, etc.) are examples of neoliberal policies for now.

Why this concern with monetary issues? Well, this is where it is important to think like a neoliberal. Neoliberals like Hayek and Friedman have a particular view of capitalism which involves the assumption that markets are both 'natural' and 'unnatural'. On the one hand, markets function best when there is no form of intervention in their operations (i.e. when they are 'free'). On the other hand, to ensure that markets can function they need to be protected from intervention, which necessitates a strong state as mentioned in the last chapter. Neoliberals like Friedman legitimate such government action by arguing that markets ensure political freedom, a perspective he extols in his book *Capitalism and Freedom*. So neoliberals have a dual concern, part economic and part moral; on the one hand, 'unfree' markets will disturb the natural functioning of markets – which depends on things like private property, individual transacting, price stability, etc. – which, on the other hand, leads to the erosion of human freedom – hence Hayek's book title *The Road to Serfdom*.

This helps to explain why neoliberals took such issue with the work of John Maynard Keynes and his emphasis on demand management and full employment. According to Richard Cockett,[12] neoliberals feared that Keynesian ideas and policies would entrench an inflationary cycle as inflation was used to control rising real wages, which were rising in response to the growing political influence of workers and trades unions. It was easier for governments to use inflation to keep *real* wages (i.e. wages minus inflation) down because wage restraints or moderation could lead to serious industrial conflicts (e.g. strikes). So, inflation helped governments meet the demands of a powerful labour movement, but depended on rising productivity and demand to ensure that the price of goods and services would fall and on the falling value of money to ensure that wages didn't rise in real terms. According to neoliberals like Hayek, however, the inflationary pressures from these wage demands of trades unions would ratchet up with no end in sight, meaning that the stability of money would be eroded leading to the collapse of markets as they would no longer be able to function properly.[13] Inevitably, governments would have to step in and assert control over wages and prices, raising fears about totalitarianism.

This account helps to explain why money and monetary policy were – and still are – so important to neoliberal thinkers across a number of schools of neoliberal thought. Of particular concern, then, is the removal of politics and politicians from any decisions relating to the money supply. According to Friedman, this lifeblood of capitalism needs to be "free from irresponsible governmental tinkering" in order to "prevent monetary policy from being subject to the day-to-day whim of political authorities".[14] Basically politicians cannot be trusted with control over the money supply because they are liable to try and appease voters by stimulating economies by increasing the money supply.

Monetary Policy: Ideas into Action?
The theoretical account above doesn't make that much sense until we understand monetary policy and how the money supply works (or doesn't). This became a particularly important debate in the 1960s and 1970s because these decades suffered from rising inflation, which the likes of Friedman had seemingly predicted. As can be seen from Figure 2.1, during the 1970s inflation rose in the USA, UK and Canada; it was also accompanied by rising unemployment leading to 'stagflation' as demand fell while prices continued to rise – this was not meant to happen from a Keynesian perspective.[15] The orthodox explanation for this crisis of the 1970s is that US government spending on the Great Society and Vietnam War along with the 1973 Oil Crisis led to rising inflation. I'll come back to why I think this is

not a complete explanation in later chapters.

FIGURE 2.1: Inflation in USA, UK and Canada (1950-2012)

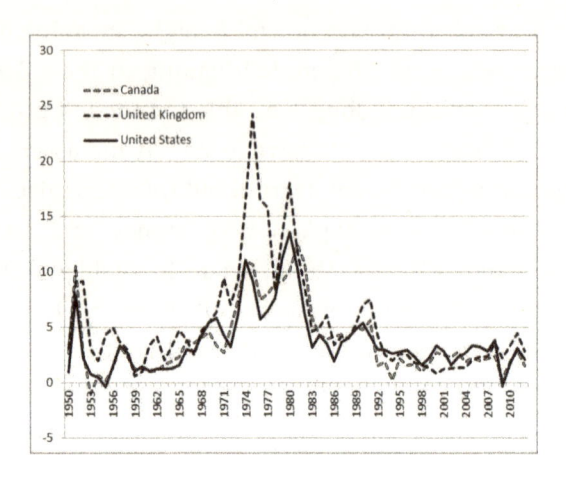

Source: OECD;[16] and Measuring Worth website.[17]

Now, it is helpful to illustrate why neoliberals made a good point, even if their explanation was rather myopic (i.e. it's the fault of government spending), as I'll explain in later chapters. To do so, however, necessitates a brief explanation of monetary theory and policy – something which is often left opaque in critical perspectives on neoliberalism. I've already mentioned it (see Box 2.1), but I probably need to do more. Monetary policy relates to the *money supply*; literally the amount of money in an economy. A good starting point for understanding this is the 2011 New Economics Foundation booklet *Where Does Money Come From?* – it provides a fairly detailed but accessible account of monetary policy and banking.[18] What might seem quite simple (e.g. money = cash in my pocket) is actually much more complicated as I'll try to explain next.

First off, there are different ways to measure money or the money supply; these are called monetary aggregates (see Box 2.2). Rather crudely they can be split between M1, M2, M3 and

M4, where each refers to a form of money which requires a certain length of time to access (e.g. instantaneously like current accounts or several months like savings accounts). What monetarists expect is that controlling the money supply will control price inflation since it will mean that no more money is allowed into circulation. Money will therefore circulate as 'naturally' required by the underlying demands of the economy – this circulation is known as the velocity of money. Thus in a booming economy, money will circulate quickly but it will be in demand as people want to use it to invest, to pay wages and to buy things meaning that money will be expensive and lenders will, therefore, be able to demand high interest rates from borrowers. The reverse is true in a recessionary economy as people seek to cut investment, wages and spending leading to falling price of money. Basically, money is treated as any other commodity by monetarists. This is where the first issue with monetarism arises; it's all about controlling the money supply but it's not clear what *type of money* – or monetary aggregate – should be controlled. Changing one type of money will lead to different effects than changing another type, as happened when policy-makers attempted to implement monetarist ideas.

Box 2.2 Definition of Monetary Aggregates

M1 = cash in our pockets plus money in current, instant-access accounts

M2 = M1 plus savings accounts that require 3-months notice

M3 = M2 plus things like repurchase agreements (repo), money market funds, debt securities and certificates of

> deposit that require longer notice periods to be redeemed as cash
>
> M4 = M3 plus other deposits
>
> **Source:** Ryan-Collins, J., Greenham, A. and Werner, R. (2011) *Where Does Money Come from: A Guide to the UK Monetary and Banking System*. London: New Economics Foundation.

Second, the starting assumption of monetarists is that any increase in money supply – whatever monetary aggregate you use – will lead to an increase in incomes and hence an increase in inflation – i.e. too much money will be chasing the same amount of goods. This is why neoliberals think it is so important to control the supply of money to an economy and why they are critical of governments which simply print more money to pay for their policies. Now, this is where things get more complex. In his 1987 book *Secrets of the Temple*, William Grieder argued that the attempted implementation of monetarism in the USA involved a rethinking of monetary policy because it necessitated the introduction of a market mechanism to determine the price of money – i.e. the interest rates on borrowing.[19] More generally, neoliberals want to institute monetarism because it involves letting markets function 'to find' the 'correct' price of money (i.e. interest rate) rather than governments setting interest rates in pursuit of government policies, whether this is full employment or inflation control. According to the theory at least, governments should establish level of money for an economy and then the market will determine the price of that money depending on demand from people who want to borrow it; as an economy grows, the government should increase the level of money. The more borrowers there are the higher interest rates will end up being.

While monetarism was a powerful idea to beat Keynesianism with, it proved an utter failure when policy-makers attempted to implement these ideas as policy. Even the so-called *Volcker Shock*, which started in 1979 and is frequently cited as a key example of neoliberalism (see Box 2.3), showed that monetarism was simply unworkable in the USA. This policy failure is reflected in the UK experience where monetarism has been described as "Thatcher's enduring failure" by Monica Prasad;[20] this is a view reiterated by others writing about Thatcher.[21] According to Greider, the expectation of American monetarists about the velocity of money proved wrong-headed in that the velocity changed depending on the political-economic situation; in Greider's words "Velocity was the Achilles' heel in Friedman's theory ... The alluring simplicity of Friedman's doctrine – control M-1 and forget about everything else – was also its central fallacy" (p.480).

Box 2.3 The *Volcker Shock*, 1979-1983

Paul Volcker was appointed as chairman of the US Federal Reserve in 1979 by President Carter; he was re-appointed by President Reagan in 1983. He was appointed to sort out rising inflation in the USA – see Figure 2.1. He attempted to implement monetarist ideas as part of a transformation of federal monetary policy to try to resolve rising inflation. What he did was try to let the market determine Federal Reserve interest rates (i.e. the base interest rate) by holding money supply and money growth constant, letting market demand for money push up or down interest rates. What happened was that interest rates were driven up sharply – see Figure 2.2 – leading to a major US recession and to

> financial crises in other parts of the world, especially Latin America, because governments had borrowed from US banks at low *real* interest rates. Inflation eventually came down but only after the impacts of rising interest rates (e.g. unemployment, recession) helped to cut inflationary pressures (e.g. wages), while shifting these inflationary pressures to assets (e.g. housing, debt, securities, etc.).
>
> **Source:** William Greider (1987) *Secrets of the Temple: How the Federal Reserve Runs the Country*. Simon & Schuster.

This policy failure resulted from the instability of the monetary aggregates themselves, since, in contrast to monetarist expectations, the velocity of these aggregates slowed down and "disrupted all the standard monetary equations" (p. 479). Thus the attempt by Federal Reserve Chairman Paul Volcker to implement monetarism during the late 1970s and early 1980s failed, even though the emphasis on controlling inflation has remained the dominant idea in central bank policy-making around the world ever since – see the 2010 paper by Geoff Mann in the journal *Progress in Human Geography* for more detail on this.[22] What this has led to is central banks targeting inflation by using interest rates which led to significant rise in government interest rates at the end of the 1970s and start of the 1980s – see Figure 2.2 for the USA and UK. These rising interest rates, especially those in the US, have had significant and long-lasting effects around the world. I'll come back to some of these impacts later in the chapter.

FIGURE 2.2: Short-term Interest Rates in USA and UK (1950-2012)

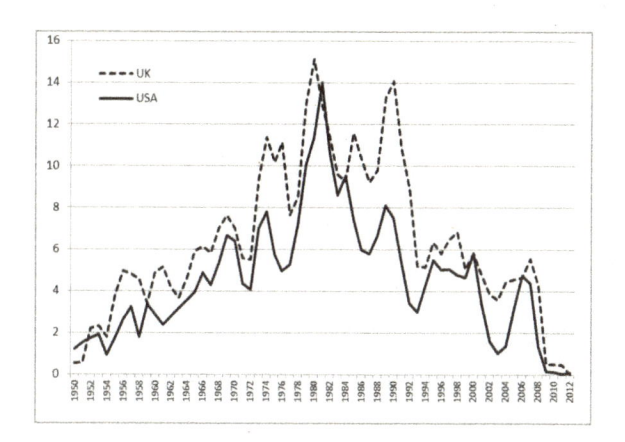

Source: Measuring Worth website.[23]

As an idea, monetarism failed. It could not be translated into policy as theorized by neoliberals like Friedman. When there were attempts to implement it, this did not lead to price stability; instead it led to changes in the velocity of money with central banks like the Federal Reserve finding that any control over monetary aggregates did not translate into the control of inflation. This does not mean that inflation lost its position as a neoliberal concern; just that central banks ended up having to use interest rates to control inflation – this led to massive interest rate rises (see Figure 2.2). While all of this may seem like a rather technical point, it's supposed to support my argument that neoliberal ideas have not necessarily translated into neoliberal policies. Ideas and policies may aim for similar outcomes but they are the former does not necessarily lead to the latter – e.g. inflation-targeting at central banks is not based on functioning money markets but on government fiat, contrary to neoliberal wishes to take government out of monetary policy.

Tight Public Spending

Monetarism and monetary policy are closely connected to government/public spending and deficits, especially in the eyes of neoliberal thinkers. First, according to neoliberals, public borrowing to finance spending is assumed to lead to rising interest rates (as they'll be less money available because the government is using it) and rising money supply (as the government will simply print more money to offset declining money availability) – see Monica Prasad and Aled Davies for discussions of the dominance of this perspective under Margaret Thatcher in the UK.[24] Second, monetarism is only possible where it is allied to changes in fiscal policy (i.e. taxation and spending) – as well as monetary policy – because government/public spending is associated with rising inflation and the attendant problems this causes; this means that monetarism necessarily seeks to influence taxation and spending policies as well. What emerges from the critical scholarship on the influence of neoliberal ideas is that these ideas promote cuts to public spending; however, this is not reflected in the evidence. Attempts to tighten government spending represent another example of how neoliberal ideas have failed to be translated into actual policies. More specifically, even governments like those of Reagan and Thatcher failed to cut public spending as originally desired (see Figures 2.3 and 2.4).

What I need to highlight in this claim is the difference between government spending and *real* government spending – these are outlined in Figures 2.3 and 2.4 below. It is obvious that government spending in the US didn't fall throughout the Reagan years; it follows a pretty steady and upward trend in Figure 2.3. When it comes to the UK, government spending falls during the 1980s, especially after 1983 when inflation and interest rates start to fall again. Now, a different picture emerges when we consider *real* government spending during the same period. When we take inflation away from government spending we can

Chapter 2. Monetarism and Fiscal Prudence vs. Ballooning Public Debt

get a more accurate picture of the actual cost of government spending, which is eroded by inflation meaning that it will ultimately cost taxpayers less to service. In looking at *real* government spending, it is evident that inflation lowered spending during the 1970s and then from 1980 onwards government spending shot up in both the USA and UK to between 30-35% of GDP. What is interesting about this is that government spending in the US actually rose from a range of 20-25% GDP before the implementation of neoliberal policies during the 1980s and beyond. Hence, it's safe to say that tight public spending has not characterized this most neoliberal of countries, nor its more junior partner in crime (UK). Next, I'm going to go over two examples to illustrate this claim before considering how these neoliberal ideas actually led to the contradictory expansion of the public debt during the height of Anglo-American neoliberalism.

FIGURE 2.3: Government Spending (%GDP) in USA and UK (1950-2012)

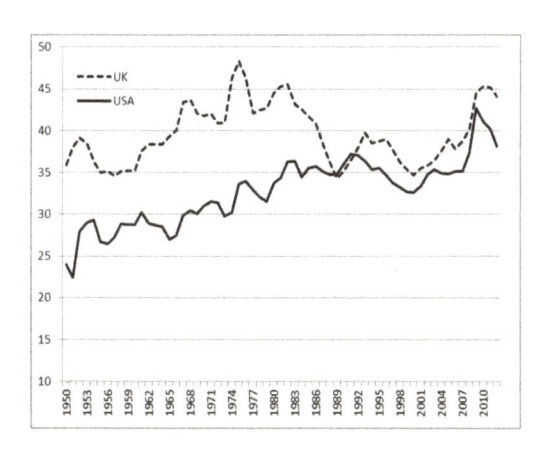

Source: *ukpublicspending.co.uk* and *usgovernmentdebt.us* (government spending).[25]

FIGURE 2.4: *Real* **Government Spending (%GDP) in USA and UK (1950-2012)**

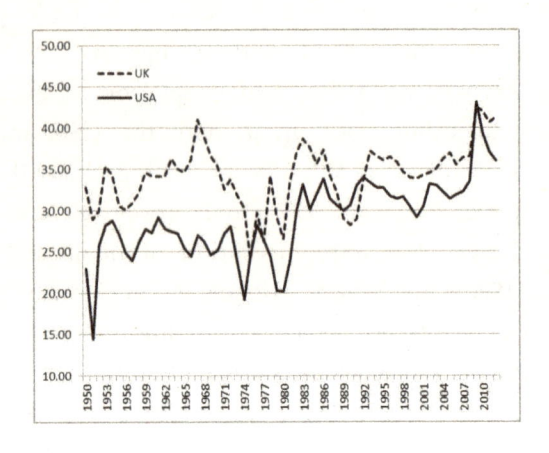

Source and notes: *ukpublicspending.co.uk* and *usgovernmentdebt.us* (government spending) (as Figure 2.3); OECD and Measuring Worth (inflation) (as Figure 2.1); *real* government spending has been calculated as government spending minus inflation from Figure 2.1.

The first example relates to the US under Reagan. Even though Federal Reserve Chair Paul Volcker tried to implement monetarism, he ended up coming into political conflict with both the Jimmy Carter and Ronald Reagan presidencies as a result of this pursuit of neoliberal ideas – see William Greider for more on this conflict. The primary reason for this was that the actions of the Federal Reserve led to negative and recessionary economic effects like rising unemployment, which neither president wanted on their watch. As the data in Figures 2.3 and 2.4 illustrate, the Reagan administration was not able to cut government spending during the first years of government. A number of factors actually compounded to make matters worse on this front including: (1) rising unemployment and need for higher welfare spending as a result; (2) tax cuts and lower government income;

Chapter 2. Monetarism and Fiscal Prudence vs. Ballooning Public Debt

and (3) rising interest rates and increasing public debt service costs. What is interesting is that Volcker came into greater conflict with Reagan's administration as time progressed, especially because of Reagan's extremely loose fiscal policy exemplified by the 1981 *Economic Recovery Tax Act* (ERTA). This policy represented a massive tax cut for businesses, but mainly for individuals according to Monica Prasad.[26] The ERTA was largely inspired and justified by supply-side theories espoused by the likes of Arthur Laffer – which Mark Blyth outlines in his book *Great Transformations*.[27] As a theory, supply-side economics was based on the assumption that tax cuts would lead to rising investment, output and incomes which would offset any lost tax income as the economy expanded. That was the theory, at least, and it was very wrong – yet another failed policy.

Funnily enough, the turn to monetarism compounded these issues, even though it was a policy failure. It meant that rising US government spending could not be reduced by simply inflating away public debt, which governments had done in the past – see Niall Ferguson's *Cash Nexus* for a detailed history of public debt and its management.[28] What resulted was a tripling of the public debt during the 1980s – at the time when the Reagan administration (rhetorically at least) espoused government spending cuts – and a doubling of the debt in *real* terms as falling inflation created a double whammy effect – see John Steel Gordon for a discussion of the US national debt.[29] See Figure 2.5 below for details of government debt during this era and afterwards.

The second example relates to the UK under Margaret Thatcher. Like Reagan, Thatcher sought to cut taxes immediately upon her electoral victory, reducing the top rate of income tax from 83% to 60% and the standard rate from 33% to 30% in the *1979 Budget*.[30] Like the US, these tax cuts were aligned with similar concerns about public spending that focused monetarist attention on the assumed equivalence between the Public Sector Borrowing Requirement (PSBR) and money supply.[31] While the attempt to institute monetarism failed in the UK like the USA, what it led to in the *1981 Budget* was a government switch to fiscal policy to control inflation through the introduction of various new taxes (e.g. excise duties) and spending cuts during a recession.[32] What followed was the decimation of British industry as whole sections of the British population were thrown onto the (employment) scrap heap as unemployment stripped communities of jobs and resources. Whether this was a deliberate political strategy is unclear, although some, like Thatcher's economic adviser Alan Budd, have suggested that:

> "The Thatcher government never believed for a moment that [monetarism] was the correct way to bring down inflation. They did however see that this would be a very good way to raise unemployment. And raising unemployment was an extremely desirable way of reducing the strength of the working classes."[33]

Like the US example outlined above then, the monetarism of Thatcher's government was only skin-deep at best. More specifically, it was very much tied to existing political preferences like reducing government spending and privatizing state-owned enterprises as part of a wider attack on the electoral base of the Labour Party. Thatcher also failed to reduce government spending for the same reasons as Reagan (e.g. rising unemployment), until the late 1980s – this represents another failed policy implementation only solved by an economic boom. Privatization, however, could be seen as a successful neoliberal idea translated into policy if we ignore certain facts. What it involved was the privatization of social housing and a range of industries from 1979 onwards (see Box 2.4), which brought much needed income into government coffers to offset tax cuts and spending rises. Arguably, the wider government policy (e.g. tax cuts) would have failed without these privatization returns and, more specifically, without the income from North Sea oil during this period.[34] Such policy failures reflect the political realities of Thatcher's control over the Conservative Party, which was always partial as evident in the failure of the monetarists to dominate the Cabinet – in fact, 'neoliberals' were largely limited to the 'economic' ministries like the Treasury (Geoffrey Howe, John Biffen), Department of Industry (Keith Joseph), Department of Trade (John Nott) and Department of Energy (David Howell).[35] It is no wonder then that Thatcher failed miserably to reduce public spending in other areas like Health (37% *real* increase during her tenure), Social Security (35%) and Education and Science (16%).[36]

Box 2.4 Privatization of State-owned Enterprises & Other Assets, UK

1979 onwards – public housing
1979, 1983, 1987 – British Petroleum
1981, 1985 – British Aerospace
1981, 1983, 1985 – Cable & Wireless
1982 – Amersham International
1982, 1985 – National Freight Corporation Britoil
1983, 1984 – Associated British Port Holdings
1984 – Enterprise Oil, Jaguar
1984, 1991, 1993 – British Telecommunications
1985 onwards – British Shipbuilders and Naval Dockyards
1986 – British Gas
1987 – British Airways, Rolls-Royce, British Airports Authority
1988 – British Steel
1989 – 10 water utilities
1990 – 12 electricity utilities

> 1991 – National Power, PowerGen, Scottish Hydro-Electric, Scottish Power
> 1992-7 – Trust Ports
> 1993 – Northern Ireland Electricity
> 1994 – British Coal
> 1996 – Railtrack, British Energy, AEA Technology
> 1996-7 – Train operating companies
>
> **Source:** David Parker (2004) *The UK's Privatisation Experiment: The Passage of Time Permits a Sober Assessment.* CESIFO Working Paper No.1126, available online: http://cyberinet03.inet-tr.org.tr/telekom/cesifo1_wp1126.pdf

Ballooning Public Debt

What the above discussion should have illustrated is that neoliberal ideas like monetarism and tightening public spending did not carry over into reality, for want of a better word – the ideas did not change the world in their own image, even if they changed the world in other ways. The policies pursued by both the Reagan and Thatcher governments did not represent either the implementation of monetarism nor public spending cuts. Rather, both monetary and fiscal policy were used to extend finance through the extension of the public debt, which grew considerably in the USA,[37] as well as the UK where it was somewhat disguised by privatization and North Sea Oil revenues. Other countries, like Canada, followed suit which explains why annual, aggregate borrowing requirements of OECD countries have risen from $100 billion in the 1970s to $650-700 billion in the 1990s.[38] These trends are evident in Figures 2.5 and 2.6 below, which show the extent to which public debt rose and fell across the Atlantic Heartland before and during the 'neoliberal' era. Again I've included a graph (Figure 2.6) to show the *real* levels of public debt in order to understand the interactions between public debt and inflation.

FIGURE 2.5: Public Debt (%GDP) in USA, UK and Canada (1970-2012)

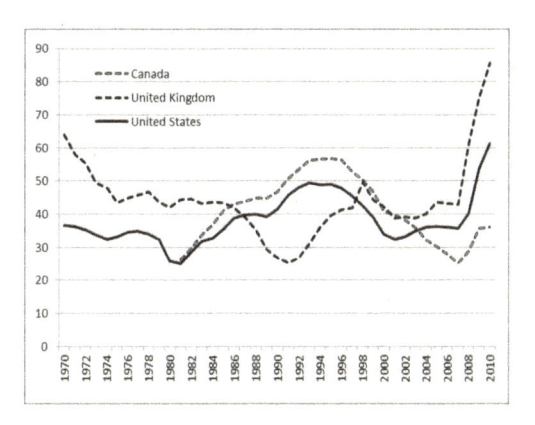

Source: OECD, *ukpublicspending.co.uk* and *usgovernmentdebt.us* (public debt).[39]

FIGURE 2.6: *Real* **Public Debt (%GDP) in USA, UK and Canada (1970-2012)**

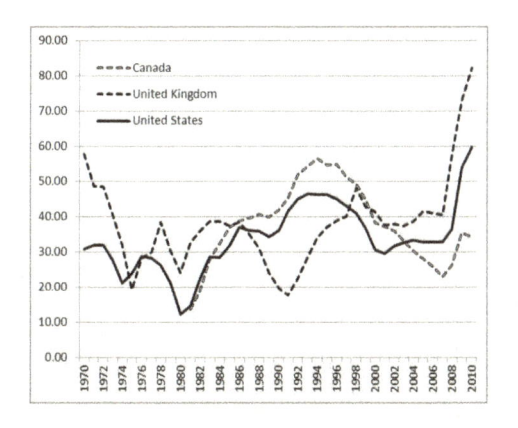

Source: OECD, *ukpublicspending.co.uk* and *usgovernmentdebt.us* (public debt) (as Figure 2.5); OECD and Measuring Worth (inflation) (as Figure 2.1).

As can be seen from Figure 2.5, the public debt of the US and Canada both rose after 1980, quite significantly and consistently until the mid-1990s; in contrast the UK's public debt fell from the mid-1980s until 1990 when it started rising. This would imply that the Thatcher government managed to reduce the public debt. However, we get a different picture if we look at *real* public debt, or public debt minus inflation. The reason to do this is, as before, that inflation erodes public debt so high public debt can be eroded by high inflation as seemingly happened in the 1970s. What Figure 2.6 shows is that across all three countries, real public debt rose from 1980 until the early 1990s (US and Canada) or late 1980s (UK). In the former case, we can see quite a ballooning of the real public debt, while the UK's goes up, down and then up again. Leaving these changes aside, what should be evident from both figures is that public debt has not declined across these three countries, despite them pursuing policies supposedly based on neoliberal ideas. One of the reasons why there was this rise in public debt is that attempts to control inflation involved raising interest rates which then reinforced rising public debt service expenses; these rose considerably during the 1980s (see Figure 2.7). What this shows is the rising interest payments on public debt in the USA, in particular, and UK, to a lesser extent, since the mid-1970s. These interest payments only fell again once *real* interest rates also began to fall (see Figure 2.8 below).

FIGURE 2.7: Interest Payments on Public Debt (%GDP) in USA and UK (1950-2012)

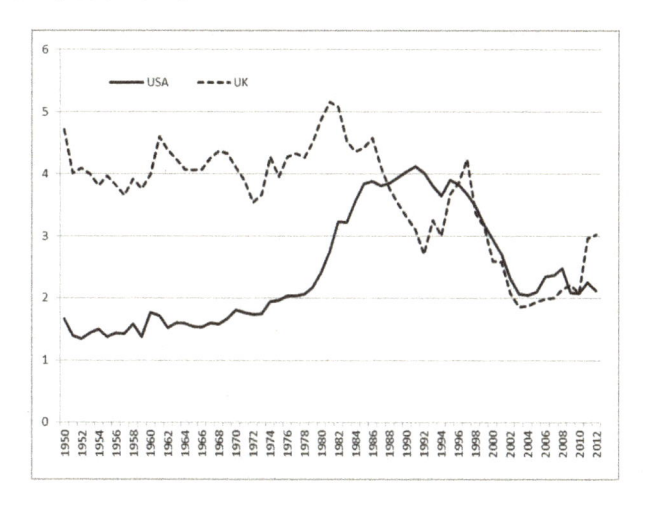

Source: *ukpublicspending.co.uk* and *usgovernmentdebt.us* (public debt interest payments).[40]

The critical issue I want to get across here is that monetarism and tight public spending both failed as policies because of the financialization of the economy (see Chapter 3), which began *before* the neoliberal turn in the late 1970s and early 1980s. The reason for this failure is critical for understanding why neoliberal ideas have had less influence on policy than we might think. Primarily it is because these ideas ran aground on the explosion of stateless, international financial markets (e.g. EuroMarkets discussed in the next chapter).[41] Here private banks essentially took over the money supply from governments through 'aggressive' lending practices – see New Economics Foundation booklet on money for more on this[42] – or, as the journalist Nicholas Shaxson, puts it:

"Monetarist theories of tackling economic problems by focusing on the money supply were coming into vogue just as the Euromarkets, lacking regulation and official checks on banks' abilities to create money out of thin air, were starting to disrupt the Fed's [and other central banks'] efforts to control that very money supply".[43]

According to the New Economics Foundation, new lending practices meant that central banks like the Federal Reserve and Bank of England lost control over the quantity of credit (i.e. amount of money) and refocused on the price of credit (i.e. cost of money, or interest rate). The prime way to influence this price was through the open market operations (OMO) of central banks – this basically involves the sale and purchase of government bonds (i.e. debt) to private banks, to either reduce the amount of money in the economy (i.e. through government bond sales that take money out of the economy) or increase it (i.e. through purchases of government bonds to push money back into the economy) – see Geoff Mann's article for more detail. The latter has been practised on a grand scale since the start of the GFC through quantitative easing. What is most important to note is that the OMO of central banks is dependent on government bonds and bond markets which raises its own problems, especially growing reliance on private investors in determining government spending and policies.

What this has all meant is that the financialization of the global economy, driven by the expansion of unregulated private bank lending, both promoted support for neoliberal ideas (e.g. monetarism and removal of government discretion over inflating away debt) and derailed the implementation of those same ideas in policy (e.g. by shifting control of money supply to private banks). The former is particularly critical in that it meant governments could no longer erode the level of public debt because they'd lost control of the money supply; therefore, the US and UK governments have ended up having to appease the demands of international financial institutions or face debilitating runs on their currencies and the consequences that result from that (e.g. capital flight).[44] This power of international, private and largely unregulated financial institutions was aptly summed up President Clinton's question while in office: "You mean to tell me that the success of the economic program and my re-election hinges on the Federal Reserve and a bunch of fucking bond traders?"[45] This has at least two major consequences I'll discuss next.

First, the capture of the money supply by private (and unregulated) banks has meant that governments have essentially lost control of their ability to reduce their public debt by inflating their economies.[46] Inflation reduces the value of debt when it is higher than interest rates – the effect is the same for other assets (e.g. housing) which is an issue I come back to in Chapter 5. This

FIGURE 2.8: *Real* **Short-term Interest Rates (%) in USA and UK (1950-2012)**

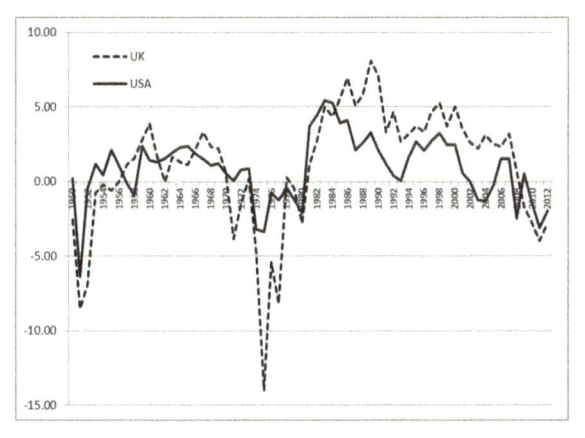

Source: OECD and Measuring Worth website (as Figures 2.1 and 2.2).

means that inflation is damaging to holders of public debt, who are therefore motivated to press governments to control inflation before they will lend. According to William Greider and Aled

Davies, this is what happened in the 1970s in the US and UK respectively as part of an 'investor revolt' – essentially lenders refusing to lend money to governments because those assets (i.e. debts) simply lost value because of inflation. This is why inflation became such a big issue in the 1970s – financial investors, including institutional investors like pension, mutual and insurance funds, faced significant declines in the value of their assets, as did individual homeowners, pensioners, etc. In order to reassure these investors governments have had to fight inflation which led to rising *real* interest rates (see Figure 2.8), which benefited investors as it increased their returns on public debt (see Figure 2.7 above).

Second, it has created a system of state-sponsored transfers of money from taxpayers to financial investors, whether these are financial elites or individual policy-holders (e.g. pensioners). This has been constructed on the back of public debt which is most obvious during the 1980s as governments tried to counteract inflation by raising interest rates, leading to significant rises in *real* interest rates and public debt interest payments (see Figures 2.7 and 2.8). Alongside tax cuts – the most easily instituted 'neoliberal' policy – and the failure to reduce government spending, all these things combined to create a perfect financial cornucopia – rising assets (from government debt), rising asset values (because of higher income streams), and more opportunities to leverage these assets through unregulated financial borrowing or lending. At the end of it all stood the taxpayer, but not the top 1% or even 10% who'd benefited from tax cuts and now benefited further from their increased lending to the government for safe and rising returns – or, as Centeno and Cohen argue, "Instead of being taxed to pay for public goods, the wealthy loaned governments money to finance deficits".[47]

Conclusion

What becomes evident when discussing the influence of

Chapter 2. Monetarism and Fiscal Prudence vs. Ballooning Public Debt

neoliberal ideas is that those ideas are often difficult to implement, especially when there are existing policy regimes built on an evolving set of principles and policies. Ideas like monetarism and tight public spending are two examples of neoliberal ideas used to support supposedly 'neoliberal' policies. Neither was successfully implemented, however, either at the time when those arguments began to dominate policy discourse nor, necessarily, later as they became increasingly accepted. For example, monetarism was never successfully implemented as theorized, although it would be possible to claim that public spending cuts have been. However, if we look at *real* public spending (i.e. public spending minus inflation) then it is actually apparent that lower public spending during the 1990s and 2000s reflects lower levels of inflation and consequently the move away from inflating away public debt.

What has mattered most during the last three or four decades is real interest rates. These helped to resolve the perceived problems of the 1970s. During 1970s, inflation rose as did interest rates, but real interest rates were negative which meant that inflation eroded the cost of the public debt. American, British and Canadian policies of the 1980s led to rising real interest rates and, consequently, rising public debt and rising public debt interest payments as inflation could no longer be used to erode this debt. In turn, this created huge demand for assets like government bonds because of the increase in income and capital gains from said assets. Inflation is, therefore, only part of the story – and not one resolved by monetarism or public spending cuts but by recession and attacks on industrial base.

In conclusion, I think it's important to emphasize that neoliberal ideas have not driven the transformations we have witnessed in our economies since the 1970s. In fact, the market instability of our and the world's economies since then stand in marked contrast to neoliberal claims that their ideas and policies will promote (market) stability. Prices may have stabilized, but fluctuations and speculation has simply shifted from price-inflation to asset-inflation as our societies have turned into asset-based economies – something I'll come back to in Chapter 4. Neoliberals like Friedman represent price-inflation as the bogeyman of economic stability, legitimating the rise of asset ownership in the form of debt, securities, housing etc. – such asset ownership has even taken on the moral overtones of individual responsibility, thriftiness, hard-work, and so on.

What is important to remember is that inflation was not curtailed by monetarism, which was not successfully implemented; rather, it was curtailed through the expansion of the public debt resulting from:

(1) Rising real interest rates;
(2) Growth of bond sales; and
(3) Borrowing from the wealthiest members of society, and the rest of us (e.g. pensions), rather than taxing them.

The one necessarily followed from the other in this process – real interest rates had to be returned to positive levels before financial investors would borrow more government debt, which was the only way to cut taxes and maintain public spending which was difficult to cut. This required more than economic ideas; it required a wholesale shift in mentality and moral outlook as well as increasing numbers of people being enrolled in Thatcher's vision of a 'property-owning democracy'. What resulted was the tying of ourselves to a massive Ponzi-scheme in which we became dependent on ever rising asset prices as asset-inflation came to replace price-inflation. It is, in this sense, not so simply as blaming the top 1% or 10% for what has happened – most of the population of the Atlantic Heartland, aside from the poorest third, has been caught up in this whirlwind of rising asset prices since the 1970s.

Chapter 2. Monetarism and Fiscal Prudence vs. Ballooning Public Debt

1. Blyth, M. (2013) *Austerity*. Oxford: Oxford University Press.
2. Prasad, M. (2006) *The Politics of Free Markets*. Chicago: University of Chicago Press.
3. Quoted in Burgin, A. (2012) *The Great Persuasion*. Cambridge, MA: Harvard University Press, p.223.
4. Blyth, M. (2002) *Great Transformations*. Cambridge: Cambridge University Press.
5. Turner, R. (2007) The 'Rebirth of Liberalism': The Origins of Neo-Liberal Ideology. *Journal of Political Ideologies* 12(1): 67-83; and, Amable, B. (2011) Morals and Politics in the Ideology of Neo-liberalism. *Socio Economic Review* 9(1): 3-30;
6. Mudge, S. 2008. What is neo-liberalism? *Socio-Economic Review* 6: 703-731
7. Bourdieu, P. (1998) Utopia of Endless Exploitation: The essence of neoliberalism. *Le Monde Diplomatique* (December) available online: http://mondediplo.com/1998/12/ 08bourdieu
8. Burgin, *The Great Persuasion*, note 3, p.105.
9. Birch, K. and Tickell, A. (2010) Making neoliberal order in the United States, in K. Birch and V. Mykhnenko (eds) *The Rise and Fall of Neoliberalism*. London: Zed Books, pp.42-59.
10. Mirowski, P. (2013) *Never Let a Serious Crisis Go to Waste*. London: Verso; also see P. Mirowski and D. Plehwe (eds) (2009) *The Road from Mont-Pèlerin: The making of the neoliberal thought collective*. Cambridge, MA: Harvard University Press.
11. Mirowski, P. (2009) The Neo-liberal Thought Collective. *Renewal* 17(4), available online: http://www.questia.com/library/1G1-237057729/the-neo-liberal-thought-collective
12. Cockett, R. (1995) *Thinking the Unthinkable: Think-tanks and the Economic Counter-revolution, 1931-1983*. London: Harper Collins Publishers.
13. Hayek, F. (1960[2011]) *The Constitution of Liberty*. London: Routledge, p.280.

14 Friedman, M. (1962[2002]) *Capitalism and Freedom*. Chicago: University of Chicago Press, p.51.
15 Blyth, *Great Transformations*, note 4.
16 Consumer Prices (MEI), available online: http://stats.oecd.org/
17 Lawrence H. Officer and Samuel H. Williamson "Annual Inflation Rates in the United States, 1775 - 2012, and United Kingdom, 1265 – 2012", MeasuringWorth, 2013, available online: http://www.measuringworth.com/inflation/
18 Ryan-Collins, J., Greenham, A. and Werner, R. (2011) *Where Does Money Come from: A Guide to the UK Monetary and Banking System*. London: New Economics Foundation.
19 Greider, W. 1987. *Secrets of the Temple: How the Federal Reserve Runs the Country*. Simon & Schuster.
20 Prasad, *The Politics of Free Markets*, note 2, p.102.
21 Young, H. (1990) *One of Us*. London: Pan Macmillan, p.203.
22 Mann, G. 2010. Hobbes' redoubt? Toward a geography of monetary policy. *Progress in Human Geography* 34(5): 601–625.
23 Lawrence H. Officer, "What Was the Interest Rate Then?" MeasuringWorth, 2013, available online: http://www.measuringworth.com/interestrates/
24 Prasad, *The Politics of Free Markets*, note 2; and, Davies, A. (2012) *The Evolution of British Monetarism: 1968-1979*. University of Oxford: Discussion Papers in Economic and Social History Number 104.
25 Available online: http://www.ukpublicspending.co.uk/spending_chart_1945_2012UKp_12c1li011mcn_F0t; and, http://www.usgovernmentspending.com/spending_chart_1950_2012USp_14s2li011mcn_F0t
26 Prasad, *The Politics of Free Markets*, note 2, pp.47-8.
27 Blyth, *Great Transformations*, note 4, pp.144-5.
28 Ferguson, N. (2002) *The Cash Nexus: Money and Power in the Modern World, 1700-2000*. London: Penguin.

Chapter 2. Monetarism and Fiscal Prudence vs. Ballooning Public Debt

29   Gordon, J. (1998) *Hamilton's Blessing: The Extraordinary Life and Times of Our National Debt*. Walker & Co.
30   Young, *One of Us*, note 21, p.148.
31   Prasad, *The Politics of Free Markets*, note 2, pp.106-111.
32   Cockett, *Thinking the Unthinkable*, note 12, p.296.
33   Quoted in Palma, J. (2009) The revenge of the market on the rentiers: Why neo-liberal reports of the end of history turned out to be premature. *Cambridge Journal of Economics* 33: p.837.
34   See, for example, Lodge, G. (2013) Thatcher and North Sea oil – a failure to invest in Britain's future. *The New Statesmen* (15 April), available online: http://www.newstatesman.com/politics/2013/04/thatcher-and-north-sea-oil-%E2%80%93-failure-invest-britain%E2%80%99s-future
35   Young, *One of Us*, note 21, pp.143-4.
36   Cockett, *Thinking the Unthinkable*, note 12, p.316.
37   According to Giovanni Arrighi the budget deficits and national debt of the US government rose between 1981 and 1991 from $74 billion to $1 trillion and from $300 billion to $4 trillion respectively; see, Arrighi, G. (1994[2010]) *The Long Twentieth Century: Money, Power and the Origins of our Times*. London: Verso, p.327.
38   Shutt, H. (2009) *The Trouble with Capitalism*. London: Zed Books, p.112.
39   Available online: http://stats.oecd.org/ (Central Government Debt); http://www.ukpublicspending.co.uk/spending_chart_1970_1979UKp_12c1li011mcn_G0t; and http://www.usgovernmentdebt.us/spending_chart_1970_1979USp_14s2li011mcn_H0f
40   Available online: http://www.usgovernmentdebt.us/spending_chart_1950_2012USp_14s2li011mcn_90t90l90f; and http://www.ukpublicspending.co.uk/spending_chart_1950_2012UKp_12c1li011mcn_90t
41   Davies, *The Evolution of British Monetarism*, note 24.

42 Ryan-Collins et al., *Where Does Money Come From*, note 18, pp.70-73.
43 Shaxson, N. (2011) *Treasure Islands: Tax Havens and the Men who Stole the World*. Bodley Head, p.130.
44 Some good work on this topic has been done by Martijn Konings and his collaborators: e.g. Konings, M. (2009) Rethinking Neoliberalism and the Subprime Crisis: Beyond the Re-regulation Agenda. *Competition and Change* 13(2): 108-127; and, Panitch, L. and Konings, M. (2009) Myths of Neoliberal Deregulation. *New Left Review* 57: 67-83.
45 Quoted in Surowiecki, J. (1999) Bonds and Domination. *New York Magazine* (1 March), available online: http://nymag.com/nymetro/news/bizfinance/columns/bottomline/199/
46 Ferguson, *The Cash Nexus*, note 28, p. 175.
47 Centeno, M. and Cohen, J. (2013) The Arc of Neoliberalism. *Annual Review of Sociology* 38: p.322; also see, Hager, S. (2013) What happened to the bondholding class? Public debt, power and the top one per cent. *New Political Economy*, available online: http://bnarchives.yorku.ca/356/

Chapter 3

Corporate Monopoly and its Neoliberal Cheerleaders

Introduction

Over the last few years I've frequently heard the comment that the US, UK and Canadian governments had to bail out their banks and financial institutions because they had become "too-big-too-fail" – or TBTF for short. How can one company or corporation be so big that we can't simply let it fail or go bankrupt? Surely that goes against everything underpinning (neoliberal) capitalism like competition, markets, etc.? Yes it does, but what politicians and policy-makers decided was that we can't let certain businesses, especially banks but also car-makers, airlines, and other companies, go bust because of the wider economic (and political) consequences. Primarily, they feared that letting one fall – as the US government did with Lehman Brothers in September 2008 and, as a result, quickly learned its lesson – would lead to a ripple effect in which business after business would then collapse. Basically, they concluded that certain businesses, especially financial ones, now formed a tightly bound and interdependent system where change in one part of the system would have disastrous knock-on effects in other parts.

The take away message from these knock-on effects is that our supposedly capitalist economy is nothing of the sort – businesses do not necessarily compete with one another, nor do they necessarily have any competitors, nor are they stopped from exerting significant influence over the market. In fact, over the last half-century or so, what we have seen is the rise of mega-corporations with massive market power able to affect prices (i.e. establish a market) without resorting to pesky competition at all. We have, rather, seen the rise of corporate monopolies contrary to the positions of those early neoliberals I discussed in Chapter 1. My purpose here, as elsewhere in this book, is to illustrate how we need to rethink neoliberalism – so, rather than assume that it is the cause of the global financial crisis (GFC), I want to argue that we might need to find another cause altogether. Put simply, my contention is that neoliberalism has not driven political-economic change over the last 40 years, it has merely legitimated it – in this sense, neoliberalism is a lapdog chasing after its master, slavishly begging for scraps from the table.

The aim of this chapter then is to illustrate this claim with a simple question: how did we get to a situation during the GFC where there were corporations 'too-big-to-fail' when the original neoliberal thinkers actually held antithetical views of such corporate monopolies and concentrations of economic power? I've already discussed this change in neoliberal thinking in Chapter 1 so what I'm going to do in this chapter is show how neoliberals not only didn't challenge corporate monopoly, they have, in fact, provided active intellectual support for it. I'm doing this to show some of the ways that neoliberalism has been shaped by other forces – that is, by corporate restructuring and the financialization of the global economy. So, rather than assume that financialization and financial crises are the *result* or *effect* of neoliberalism or a neoliberal, class-based project, I'm going to argue the reverse – what we now know as neoliberalism is better defined as a financialized system of corporate monopoly. I'll do this by outlining the rise of international financial markets and then by examining the concentration of corporate power and the rise of corporate monopolies. Then I'll show how this organizational transformation has been championed and legitimated by changes in the perspective of thinkers from the second Chicago school as they came to support and promote corporate monopoly. Throughout, my intention is to go beyond the class-based analyses of neoliberalism, which I'll outline at the beginning of the chapter.

Chapter 3. Corporate Monopoly and its Neoliberal Cheerleaders

What is Neoliberalism III: Class-based Project?

The third critical perspective on neoliberalism I want to consider is one of the most common, and finds its clearest expression in the work of Marxists scholars like the geographers David Harvey and Richard Peet as well as heterodox economists like Gérard Duménil and Dominique Lévy.[1] The starting point for this critique of neoliberalism is the claim it is a project to restore the power of economic elites – basically, it's a class-based analysis.[2]

Box 3.1 The Washington Consensus

Arising in the 1980s, the Washington Consensus is a term coined by economist John Williamson to describe the international development policies promoted by international financial institutions like the World Bank and International Monetary Fund along with the US government. Although Williamson didn't originally mean the term to be negative, it has since taken on negative connotations and is especially associated with structural adjustment programmes (or SAPs). Basically it involves the promotion of free market reforms, including: tight fiscal discipline; cuts in public subsidies and public spending; tax cuts; capital and trade liberalization; privatization; deregulation; private property rights; etc.

Source: Richard Peet (2007) *The Geography of Power*. London: Zed Books.

From this perspective, neoliberalism is characterized as both a political and economic project because it involves the enrolment of the state in the restoration of class power and the reorientation of the economy to the benefit of economic elites. It is both concerned with individual countries, like the work of Duménil and Lévy on the USA,[3] as well with the globalization of neoliberal principles through the Washington Consensus outlined by Richard Peet and others (see Box 3.1).

It is instructive to start with Harvey's analysis because he represents a key critic of neoliberalism.[4] His main point is that the economic crisis of the 1970s – which I've already mentioned in previous chapters – was used by economic elites to restore their wealth and income, which had been eroded by the post-WW2 consensus. According to Harvey this involved various mechanisms – covering privatization, commodification, financialization and state redistribution – to 'dispossess' workers, consumers, citizens and others of their wealth and incomes. What resulted was a reversal of the gains made by average workers since WW2 as elites captured any further gains from growth after the 1970s, while workers experienced stagnant wages. Harvey's analysis draws heavily on the early work of Duménil and Lévy in their book *Resurgent Capital* – they basically make the same argument as Harvey, which they reinforced in their 2011 book *The Crisis of Neoliberalism*. In this later book, Duménil and Lévy argue that financialization has led to an alliance between capitalists and corporate managers, such that neoliberalism can be defined as the "second financial hegemony". All of this, of course, came to a shuddering halt with the GFC, although it's still not clear whether any progressive outcomes will occur from the crisis or not.

Much of this Marxist analysis is taken up with identifying how neoliberalism has benefited particular economic classes, especially economic elites, by using data on the concentration of wealth and income to show rising inequality. As critics of neoliberalism, these writers characterize neoliberalism as a class-based project constituted by ideological discourses, social forces and state apparatus. For example, Bastiaan van Apeldoorn and Henk Overbeek argue that this includes "a mix of pro-market and

Chapter 3. Corporate Monopoly and its Neoliberal Cheerleaders

supply-side discourses (laissez faire, privatization, liberalization, deregulation, competiveness) and monetarist orthodoxy (price stability, balanced budgets, austerity)".[5] Again, I've probably butchered the intellectual value of these thinkers in my brief synopsis here – my apologies to the authors and readers alike. What I'd suggest is reading the work of people like David Harvey – especially his *Brief History of Neoliberalism* – and Duménil and Lévy for a general overview. Others to read would include Bastian van Apeldoorn for a specifically European view and Richard Peet on the Global South.

To end my overview I want to highlight how these critics explicitly link neoliberalism with the financialization of the economy, primarily because the former involves the promotion of particular concerns beneficial to the financial sector (e.g. liberalization, deregulation, price stability, etc.). While this provides a good illustration of what has happened over the last 30-40 years – especially the rise of the top 1% – what it's less good at is identifying *specifically* neoliberal processes or how *specifically* neoliberal policies have led to those changes and the transformation of our societies. Crudely, there is a sense that these scholars assume that neoliberalism (i.e. something we can identify as having a negative impact) happened because of the outcome (i.e. inequality).[6] Moreover their association of neoliberalism with financialization fails to acknowledge that the latter has its origins well before the rise of neoliberalism and actually contrasts with neoliberalism in important ways, one of which I highlighted in the introduction – that is, the notion that there are businesses too big for governments to let fail and, therefore, effectively not operating under market conditions.

Financialization and the Re-emergence of International Finance

So why is this of any importance to us now? Well, since the end of WW2 the global economy has both expanded – in that more countries are tied into global trade and investment flows – and got smaller in that fewer and fewer economic actors (e.g. multinational corporations) play the tunes we all dance to. The work of Peter Dicken provides a helpful introduction to these trends should you want to explore them in more depth.7 What I want to cover here are two such trends; (a) the expansion and concentration of financial markets, often referred to as financialization, and (b) the rise of monopolistic corporations as key economic actors. Both of these trends have been ably supported by deliberate government policies, which have also been blamed for the GFC. I'll address the first issue in this section and then come onto the second issue in the following section.

Financialization as a Neoliberal Class Project?
Many leftist commentators, intellectuals and activists have made a direct connection between neoliberalism and the GFC. They have made a direct link between neoliberal ideas, policies and politics and the *financialization* (see Box 3.2) of the Atlantic Heartland economies – i.e. USA, UK and Canada, as well as other countries like Ireland, Iceland, etc. Financialization is a term increasingly used to define what has happened in these economies because it reflects the dominance of the financial sector whether in terms of profits, revenues, proportion of economy, employment, etc. More generally, a number of scholars have argued that the investment, management and movement of money (or capital) are replacing the production of physical goods and services as the key source of economic expansion and ultimately growth.[8] In broader terms, what this means is that centres of finance like the City of London, Wall Street and Bay Street have come to dominate policy discourse across these Heartland countries while other regions or industries are left to languish or pick up the leftovers.

> **Box 3.2 What is Financialization?**
>
> Financialization is the growing dominance of the financial sector over the direction of the economy. The financial sector is sometimes classified as the FIRE sector (i.e. finance, insurance, real estate) and consists of institutions like commercial and investment banks, institutional investors (e.g. pension, mutual and insurance funds), equity investors (e.g. hedge funds), and mortgage providers. As Greta Krippner (2005) highlights, there are different ways to identify the dominance of finance in the economy – e.g. employment, profits, revenues, proportion of economy, etc.
>
> **Source:** Greta Krippner (2005) The financialization of the American economy. *Socio-Economic Review* 3: 173-208.

As mentioned, leftist scholars like David Harvey, Duménil and Lévy, and others mentioned previously often explicitly link financialization with neoliberalism. I'll go through a few examples here for illustration purposes. First, Harvey defines neoliberalism as a political project to restore the "power of economic elites" through *accumulation by dispossession*, which entails the financialization of the economy.[9] More recently, Harvey argued that financialization is a way to redistribute income and wealth upwards, primarily through the credit (and debt) system.[10] Second, in their earlier work Duménil and Lévy (2004) argue – like Harvey – that financialization is part of a neoliberal project to restore the hegemony of financial elites. In their most recent book, *The Crisis of Neoliberalism*, they claim that neoliberalism is a "second financial hegemony" in which financial instruments (e.g. CDOs, CDSs, etc.) have reached "unprecedented levels of sophistication and expansion".[11] For these leftist scholars and others, financialization has led inexorably to the concentration of income and wealth in the richest sections of society (e.g. the top 1%), supporting a return to levels of inequality not seen since the Gilded Age at the turn of the twentieth century (see Figure 3.1). These writers emphasize the claim that neoliberalism and finance are bound at the hip; as such it makes sense to talk about neoliberal finance or neoliberal financialization and their dual responsibility for rising inequality. While these arguments are convincing, it is evident by now that I think they miss an important part of the puzzle. As usual, I'm not the only person making such claims; for example, Sandy Hager has argued that these critical perspectives miss the conflict going on between different parts of the finance sector (e.g. investment banks vs. commercial banks).[12]

FIGURE 3.1: Income Inequality in USA, UK and Canada (1908-2011)

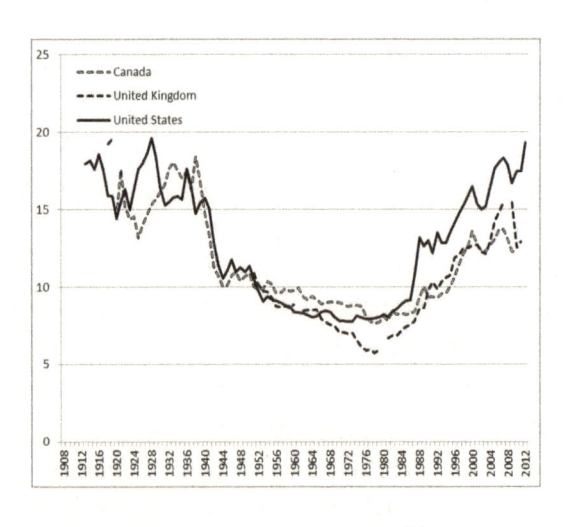

Source: The World Top Incomes Database.[13]

Linking financialization to a neoliberal project to restore class

Chapter 3. Corporate Monopoly and its Neoliberal Cheerleaders

power misses more than it illuminates. My concern here is that the focus on *neoliberal finance* – as shorthand for these critical claims about the link between neoliberalism and financialization – does not address how a diverse range of people, groups and organizations were enrolled in the expansion of finance since the 1970s, leading to the wholesale transformation of our economies as they have shifted towards an asset-based system. I come back to these issues in Chapter 4 when I focus on the assetization of the economy and what this means for 'average' people and for the top 1%. For now, what I want to highlight is the need to look at organizational change, not just class politics. This is especially relevant as corporations have increased in size and dominance, *extending* corporate monopolies around the world. Before explain what I mean by that, however, I'm going to argue that financialization has actually originated independently of any neoliberal project, ran counter to it in many cases, and helped to re-shape neoliberalism in its own image as an 'organizational project' driven by changes in corporate strategy as opposed to a class interests.

The Re-emergence of International Financial Markets

The key point I want to get across here is that financialization doesn't equal neoliberalism – moreover, I don't think they can be equated as two sides of a class-based project. There are two main reasons for my claim. First, in thinking about financialization we need to trace back to its origins to see whether neoliberalism is implicated in these origins. I don't think neoliberalism is relevant to the origins of financialization as I'll show below; specifically, what we might think of contemporary neoliberalism (i.e. second Chicago school) was a peripheral set of ideas, policies etc. until the crisis of the 1970s while financialization has its roots earlier in the 1950s and 1960s (if not before). Second, we have to think about *how* neoliberalism is implicated in financialization – before the 1970s it would be problematic to equate the emergence of international financial markets with a specific neoliberal project or even set of policies. It would be more apt, in fact, to argue that financialization (or the re-emergence of international financial markets – see Eric Helleiner on this)[14] arose as a consequence of Keynesian policies. In order to illustrate these two claims I'm going to outline when and how the international financial markets that now dominate our lives emerged.

The origins of financialization can be traced back to the so-called Euromarkets, which arose in the late 1950s and early 1960s – Gary Burns provides a very helpful and detailed account of their origins in London and a pretty clear definition (see Box 3.2). It is in these two decades that we can see international financial markets *re-emerge* as important influences and drivers on business and government activity. The fact that they are "re-emerging" also implies that they are not 'neoliberal'. The Euromarkets are state-less (i.e. technically offshore) financial markets that consist of two elements: (1) Eurocurrency markets and (2) Eurobond markets. The first of these entails deposits and the latter the loans made with these deposits. The reason for their emergence in the late 1950s is complicated but generally relates to attempts by banks and other businesses to avoid capital controls instituted as part of the Bretton Woods system (BWS) after WW2. In particular, American corporations needed to find ways to use the profits generated from their international activities, since repatriating those profits to the US would lead to losses because of limits on interest payable on deposits (so-called Regulation Q) – a paper by Leo Panitch and Martijn Konings is very useful for understanding this.[15] Thus the Euromarkets involves holding *and* lending dollars outside of the US, which was far more profitable than moving those dollars back to the US.

Chapter 3. Corporate Monopoly and its Neoliberal Cheerleaders

---

Box 3.2 What are Euromarkets?

The Euromarkets are where 'Euro-currencies' are deposited and lent. According to Gary Burns, "The prefix 'Euro' is a misnomer, in that it defines what is an *offshore currency*, held and used *outside* the country where it acts as legal tender, and traded in a market which exists outside the system of state-prescribed banking jurisdiction."

Source: Gary Burns (1999) The state, the City and the Euromarkets. *Review of International Political Economy* 6(2): p.226 [emphasis in original].

What these Euromarkets led to was a massive growth in deposits *and* lending outside of any government jurisdiction; this had a major impact on the ability of governments to maintain capital exchange controls as they could not control this money or demand that lenders hold specific levels of capital reserves. In fact, the Euromarkets led to the US and UK relaxing (and then abandoning) their capital controls in the 1970s as neither government was able to ameliorate the impact of a financial funds that surpassed world reserves by 1975.[16] The expansion and size of the Euromarkets has meant that they quickly eroded the ability of the American and British governments to control, first, their exchange rates and, then, their money supply, both of which they ended up ceding to international financial investors who make decisions based on speculative expectations about what governments are going to do next.[17] The power these international financial markets embody is illustrated in the size of the Euromarkets, which is shown in Figure 3.2. As you can see from the graph, the Euromarkets topped $1 trillion in 1980 by which point they had surpassed government reserves around the world,[18] representing about 1/18 of world GDP – this phenomenal rise hasn't stopped as by the year 2000 the Euromarkets represented nearly ¼ of world GDP.

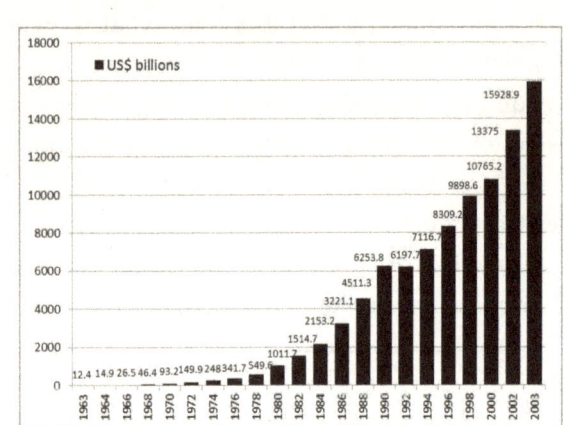

FIGURE 3.2: The Expansion of the Euromarkets

Year	US$ billions
1963	12.4
1964	14.9
1966	26.5
1968	46.4
1970	93.2
1972	149.9
1974	248
1976	341.7
1978	549.6
1980	1011.7
1982	1514.7
1984	2153.2
1986	3221.1
1988	4511.3
1990	6253.8
1992	6197.7
1994	7116.7
1996	8309.2
1998	9898.6
2000	10765.2
2002	13375
2003	15928.9

Source: Adapted from Keith Philbeam (2013) *International Finance*. Basingstoke: Palgrave Macmillan.[19]

Now, my point is that the emergence of these Euromarkets is what drove much of the regulatory changes we see in countries like the US, UK and Canada during the 1970s and 1980s (see Box 3.3). These changes weren't the *result* of a neoliberal class-based project, as much as they were the outcome of a half-implemented, Keynesian BWS. Basically, the BWS led to a shift from foreign portfolio investment (i.e. purchases of foreign debt, securities, etc.) to foreign direct investment (i.e. investment in physical assets) because of constraints on the movement of capital. This meant that American multinationals corporations (MNCs) couldn't repatriate their profits as desired, so they ended up creating the Euromarkets as a way to avoid capital controls and other regulations, while continuing to invest and return a profit on their capital. These were not neoliberal class-based goals as

Chapter 3. Corporate Monopoly and its Neoliberal Cheerleaders

such, nor did the Euromarkets arise from neoliberal policies – for example, and as mentioned in previous chapters, what we think of as neoliberalism was still not a stable set of ideas or policies at the time (i.e. 1950s and 1960s). Rather, the Euromarkets emerged as a result of MNCs trying to bypass the BWS leading to the loss of control by the American and British governments – amongst others – of their money supply as private suppliers of money ended up outside of government oversight. According to Yanis Varoufakis, this ballooning dollar glut gradually benefited the US because it meant that the US could run a twin deficit (trade and budget), attracting surplus dollars from around the world that had built up in the Euromarkets as a consequence of capital controls – once these controls were abolished in the 1970s all this money flooded into the US to support the expansion of financialization, securitization, etc. through investment in public, corporate and household debt.[20]

Box 3.3: The Deregulation and Re-regulation of Finance

USA
- 1974 capital controls abolished (imposed in 1963)
- 1978 foreign banks under federal regulations
- 1980 lowered bank reserve requirements and started phase-out of interest rate limits
- 1982 deregulation of interest rate restrictions (e.g. *Regulation Q*) and credit controls (e.g. Savings & Loans)

UK
- 1971 *Competition and Credit Control* – reserve ratios reduced to 12.5%
- 1975 capital controls eased
- 1979 capital controls abolished

- 1981 compulsory reserve ratios abolished
- 1981 banks allowed to compete with building societies

Canada
- 1974 although not imposed properly, capital controls abolished
- 1980 foreign banks of certain size allowed to compete

Source: John Williamson and Molly Mahar (1998) *A Survey of Financial Liberalization*. Princeton University: Essays in International Finance No.211; Matt Taibbi (2011) *Griftopia*. New York: Spiegel and Gau Trade Paperbacks; Hager, S.B. (2012) Investment Bank Power and Neoliberal Regulation: From the Volcker Shock to the Volcker Rule, in H. Overbeek and B. van Apeldoorn (eds) *Neoliberalism in Crisis*. Basingstoke: Palgrave Macmillan, pp. 68-92.

Corporate Monopoly and Its Neoliberal Cheerleaders

When looking at a topic it is often interesting to find out how much or how little attention has been paid to it. The easiest way to do this is through a simple database or internet search. In researching this book I found that one area where there seems to be limited data and just as limited amount of research is corporate monopoly – e.g. how have monopoly levels changed over time? What has this meant for our economies? Etc. These are critical questions, especially as they relate to the increasing concentration of economic power in fewer and fewer hands and the corresponding emergence of financial institutions that are 'too-big-to-fail'. Instead of thorough study, however, these sorts of issues are rarely rigorously theorized by critical writers; more frequently, things like corporate monopoly are characterized in vague terms as 'corporate power'.[21] What I want to do next is

Chapter 3. Corporate Monopoly and its Neoliberal Cheerleaders

provide a clearer outline of corporate monopoly and discuss how this relates to neoliberalism – or, more accurately, does not.

Corporate Monopoly
Most of us at some stage or another have played the board-game *Monopoly®* where we try to collect properties, build hotels and construct monopolistic positions so that we can bankrupt other players. We can understand these fairly simple dynamics of the game – we try to win by dominating the board. Funnily enough, the game supposedly started out in the early 1900s as a way to illustrate the dangers of monopolies – see the 2006 book Philip Orbanes called *Monopoly: The World's Most Famous Game & How it Got that Way*. It was, at least in part, a response to the monopoly practices of the Robber Baron era at the end of the nineteenth century when 'capitalists' like Rockefeller, Carnegie, Morgan etc. sought to dominate whole industries. More direct responses to these monopolies included legislation in the USA like the *Sherman Anti-trust Act* (1890) designed to stop such anti-competitive practices.

Nowadays corporate monopoly and the concentration of corporate power are yet again in evidence. Some recent work by three physicists, Vitali, Glattfelder and Battiston, shows how networked and inter-locking connections between multinational corporations (MNCs) have led to the (global) concentration of corporate control. These physicists demonstrate that only 737 MNCs control 80% of the value of global MNCs and that 147 control 40% – such figures illustrate the importance of corporate monopoly as a topic today.[22] Looking at industrial and commercial sector after sector, we can see evidence of monopolies dominating our economies – it is almost like we have gone back to the late 1800s. However, it would be wrong to claim that this is a recent phenomenon or concern since leftist criticism of monopoly stretches back to at least the 1950s and 1960s when people like Paul Baran and Paul Sweezy published *Monopoly*

Capital.[23] One example of recent analysis – of the little that has been done – is the work of John Bellamy Foster and colleagues in the *Monthly Review*.[24] What they show is that:

- The number of US manufacturing industries where the top 4 companies account for 50% of "shipment value" declined from 1947 (30%) to 1987 (25%) but has since risen to about 40% of industries.
- The revenues of the top 200 US corporations have risen to nearly 30% of total business revenues (from 21% in 1950).
- The gross profits of the top 200 US corporations have risen to 30% of total gross profits (from 13% in 1950).

What more recent critics point out is that there are now more explicit linkages between big business and government. Naomi Klein argues in *The Shock Doctrine*, for example, that "what has emerged is a powerful ruling alliance between a few very large corporations and a class of wealthy politicians".[25] According to Klein, this alliance is not capitalist, it is corporatist – basically, government and corporations now run the economy to the benefit of private business. All of this, moreover, is hidden behind a facade of free market rhetoric propounded by Chicago school thinkers like Milton Friedman whose "vision coincided precisely with the interests of large multinationals" (p.66). In the end, Klein is making a very explicit claim that the state and business have become one and the same – the former is enrolled and conflated with the interests of the latter.

Whether or not we accept Klein's argument, it is important look at the extent of big business and corporate monopoly in the contemporary world – have economies of scale, for example, become monopolies of scale? Big business is getting bigger, there is no doubt; the question then is whether it is becoming more monopolistic. It is obviously important not blur these two things. While there are some very large multinationals (MNCs), they are

Chapter 3. Corporate Monopoly and its Neoliberal Cheerleaders

not necessarily monopolies as well. However, they still might have enormous market power since MNCs are characterized by the functional integration of (outsourced) production and distribution across national borders – see Peter Dicken's book *Global Shift*.[26] This market power can mean that MNCs exert power over their suppliers (e.g. quality assurance), distributors (e.g. supply chain management), consumers (e.g. advertising), and even governments as they can threaten to move their facilities to countries with the least regulation, lowest taxation, etc. – this had been called regulatory arbitrage. One clear example of this market power is Wal-Mart which Charles Fishman discusses in his book *The Wal-Mart Effect*.[27] It's not just Wal-Mart either; an interesting graph in *The Economist* magazine shows that the largest US companies have increased in size over the last 15 years or so. For example, the assets of the largest 50 US firms represented about 70% GDP in 1996, which has since risen to about 130% GDP in 2011.[28] Such economies of scale all too easily turn into monopolies of scale.

In contrast to market power, monopoly represents the dominance of a particular sector by a small number of businesses. It does not mean, however, control or dominance by *one* business. It's helpful to consider the work of Barry C. Lynn here; he's written about modern monopolies in his book *Cornered*.[29] His basic argument is that there has been a shift in competition from the horizontal plane (i.e. between competing firms) to the vertical plane as large corporate monopolies now compete with everyone below them (e.g. workers) for society's wealth. This concentration of industrial and commercial sectors hit a peak in 2006, just before the GFC, when mergers and acquisitions in the US reached a new record of $3.8 trillion (p.8). While his argument might be contentious, Lynn does point out a really important issue which is often hidden behind a wall of brand names, marketing and advertising. Production and manufacturing are now largely outsourced, globally in most cases, and carried out by a limited number of suppliers who we've never even heard of. The systemic inter-dependence between these suppliers and more well-known corporations is outlined in his previous book, *End of the Line*, where Lynn claimed, for example, that almost all semiconductors are manufactured by only two Taiwanese companies.[30] He provides other examples in *Cornered* – so, while everything from cement to toothpaste are dominated by a few brand-name firms, the production or manufacturing underpinning these companies has also become concentrated in fewer and fewer hands. As a result we've ended up with an economic system that is incredibly vulnerable to shocks, of whatever sort, as anything that affects these unknown suppliers ripples out across the economy.

This all started some time ago, however, and not with neoliberalism. As countries like the US, UK and Canada changed their company law and regulations during the 1800s, large corporations emerged as finance enabled the centralization of capital leading to a 'corporate revolution'.[31] What this revolution unleashed has not only been beneficial in some respects – e.g. efficiencies from economies of scale – it has also led to the extension of market power over other firms, citizens and consumers, as well as governments. All of this is inherent in the corporate organizational structure; these large corporations seek to become monopolies because it will mean there is no competition to reduce their profits – you can charge what you like when no one else sells what you sell. Monopoly is, therefore, very much part of corporate capitalism, as are the threats it presents, especially to competitive markets as many neoliberals highlighted in the early- to mid-twentieth century (see Chapter 1). It is, therefore, rather surprising that corporate monopoly is now the norm in supposedly free, competitive and liberal market economies like the USA, UK and Canada. Going back to the idea of TBTF, it is surprising that the concentration of the finance sector has been accompanied by so little protest from supposedly

Chapter 3. Corporate Monopoly and its Neoliberal Cheerleaders

free market advocates; this is even more surprising considering the comments of Milton Friedman back in the 1970s:

> "If I said to you, 'Here I've got a major sector of the economy in which no enterprise ever fails, no one ever goes broke,' you would tell me, 'My god, there must not be any competition here.'" Friedman said. "That's correct. The banking industry has been a highly protected, sheltered industry. That's because banks have been the constituency of the Federal Reserve."[32]

In fact, since the 1970s supposedly free market advocates like Friedman have become very comfortable with corporate monopoly – they have largely reversed their earlier position and become the biggest cheerleaders of large corporations, even corporate monopolies. This has led Colin Crouch to describe the 'neoliberal era' as the "corporate takeover of the market".[33] I'll come back to Crouch's arguments shortly, but I want to presage what I argue next with a question; namely, how did this *second corporate revolution* happen? My answer is that it is the effect of another important trend over the same period – the rise of intangible assets and intangible values – discussed in Chapter 4. This trend is tied into the financialization of corporations themselves over the twentieth century and helps to illustrate why class-based analyses can only go so far when trying to explain the concentration (and consequent inequalities) of wealth and value in our economies.

Neoliberal Cheerleaders
In his book *The Strange Non-death of Neoliberalism* Colin Crouch, like much recent and critical scholarship on neoliberalism, identifies a key shift in the attitude of neoliberals, especially those in the Chicago school, towards anti-trust legislation and regulation. The basic premise of his argument is neoliberals

accept that markets are dependent on rules and laws that institute and enforce competition – in this sense competitiveness is not a natural or inherent characteristic of human behaviour. What Crouch is laying out here are the assumptions of neoliberal thinkers stretching back to the seminal meeting in Paris in 1938 – basically, markets need to be made *and* protected.[34] What is at stake according to these early neoliberals is the protection of market competition; other benefits will flow from competitive market exchange – see, for example, the arguments of both Hayek and Friedman in their popularizations of markets.

Now, in Chapter 3 of his book, Crouch argues that corporations have taken over the market as they have grown larger, first as they globalized and then as they cannibalized each other towards the end of the twentieth century. What he claims is that corporations have managed to take over the market as a result of 'neoliberal' theories criticizing anti-trust regulation. The second Chicago school comprised not only economists, but also legal and management theorists. In combining these three different areas of research, Chicagoans built a picture of the world in which antitrust regulation came to represent a negative activity detrimental to consumer welfare. Back in Chapter 1 I already mentioned the transformation of neoliberal thinking on monopoly; this is where it matters. Basically, in the 1950s various Chicago school academics studied the effects of monopoly and came to the conclusion that it wasn't actually that bad for the economy – by which they meant it didn't create inefficiencies because it didn't interfere with consumer welfare. Consumer welfare, defined primarily as cheap prices, replaced consumer choice as the key issue of concern, meaning that corporate monopoly is no longer an issue *if* it enables the production of consumer products more cheaply than many firms competing against each other.[35]

It was the convergence of law and economics that led to this re-evaluation of corporate monopolies and anti-trust regulation. It wasn't an instantaneous change, instead happening over much of the 1970s and 1980s. Nor has it necessarily finished since there are ongoing conflicts about corporate size as evident in the notion of TBTF. One of the most interesting discussions of the transformation of anti-trust law is a 2010 paper by Will Davies in the journal *Economy and Society*.[36] He discusses its origins in price theory – the whole basis of Chicago economics – and the application of price theory to non-economic matters (e.g. law). Much of the theory underpinning these arguments is derived from work on transaction cost economics done by economist Ronald Coase, especially his 1937 article "The nature of the firm" (see Box 3.4 below). Price theory and its implications influenced and were taken up in the work of legal scholars like Richard Posner and Robert Bork, who were later appointed as judges by Ronald Reagan. According to Davies, as a result of their ideas and arguments support for anti-trust enforcement fell and the legal perspectives shifted as lawyers, judges, etc. adopted economic efficiency as a more important criterion in anti-trust decisions than any normative position. Davies' arguments here are reiterated by those of Colin Crouch and by Foster et al.

Box 3.4 Ronald Coase and Transaction Costs

In a now famous 1937 article, Ronald Coase asked a fairly simple question – if markets are the most efficient way to match people's individual interests then why are their business firms? Surely if the market was efficient then there would be no firms? This led him to theorize that actually when people engage in market exchange they face transaction costs (e.g. costs to exchange like costs of information) – this could include the costs of negotiating, monitoring and enforcing a contract. So, it can be more efficient to organize economic activity in organizations because they

> can reduce transaction costs. For example, imagine having to arrange a new contract every time you want someone to make something for you; it would be easier to hire them on a long-term contract to make things instead.
>
> **Source:** Ronald Coase (1937) The Nature of the Firm. *Economica* 4(16): 386–405.

What this discussion is meant to illustrate is that second Chicago school ideas helped to transform law and anti-trust policy thereby encouraging and facilitating the emergence of corporate monopolies. That they did so in the name of free markets is beside the point, as is the reversal of perspective from earlier neoliberals (see Chapter 1). What does matter is that people like Bork and Posner supported corporate monopoly because of, and not despite, their assumptions about free markets and competition. In fact, they were able to rationalize this apparent contradiction with reference to theories that have been used to characterize corporations as simply a 'nexus of contracts' and not an independent entity.[37] Part of the reason for the influence of these Chicago school ideas is that they found a ready audience for their work in the finance sector which was seeking to extend its influence over other sectors at precisely the time that people like Bork and Posner were proselytizing their ideas. The sanitizing of corporate monopoly meant that financial institutions and individual financiers could legitimate the mergers wave in the 1970s and predominantly 1980s,[38] as well as the subsequent astronomical rise in market capitalization (see Figure 3.3). The rise of public equity markets in both USA and UK after 1980 is directly related to Crouch's point that this rethinking of corporate monopoly favoured "the emergence of giant corporations" based on the assumption that this "will always lead to improved efficiency".[39]

FIGURE 3.3 Share Indexes in USA (right) and UK (left) (1950-2012)

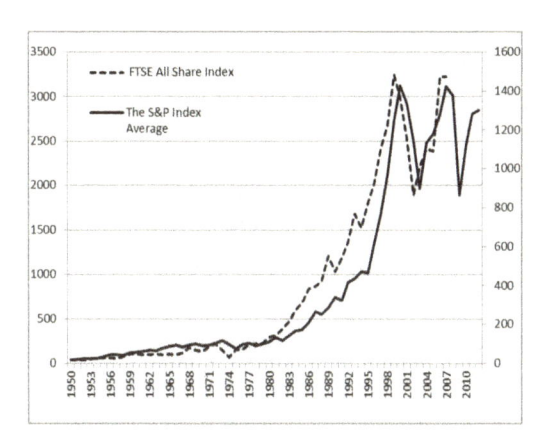

Source: Measuring Worth (S&P Index Average); and Finfacts Ireland (FTSE All Share Index).[40]

Whatever my argument, what is important to note is that corporate monopoly is *not* an effect of either neoliberal ideas or some form of neoliberal class-based project. Although the likes of Naomi Klein and Colin Crouch specifically align neoliberalism with corporate monopoly and power, what they both fail to acknowledge is that these two things have been around for a long time, well before the 1980s, 1970s or even 1960s – that is, well before any neoliberal or class-based project emerges. In fact, Stephen Wilks recently pointed out that the likes of John Kenneth Galbraith identified oligopoly as a defining characteristic of the US economy way back in 1952 in the book *American Capitalism*.[41] Similar claims are made by Baran and Sweezy in the 1960s who trace back the idea of monopoly to Rudolf Hilferding in the early twentieth century. Thus corporate monopoly has a much longer history than neoliberalism and is more likely to have driven the transformation of neoliberal ideas during the

1950s, 1960s and 1970s than the other way round. That is, neoliberalism didn't promote the rise of corporate monopolies, championed by a new wave of radical thinking bubbling up from the offices of economists and others at the University of Chicago; instead, existing corporate monopolies led neoliberals to seek ways to defend corporate monopoly against attacks by New Deal advocates, socialists and the likes.

Corporate Monopoly and the Concentration of Financial Assets

In the next chapter I'm going to return to some specifics of organizational restructuring, and consider whether they have either been engendered by free market ideas or influenced the emergence of those ideas, especially the work of scholars at the Chicago school of business. Why? Well, critics of neoliberalism rarely focus on the work of business schools in reproducing a particular form of capitalism, tending instead to focus on the work of economics. Although business schools have become increasingly dominated by neoclassical economics, it is notable that the management thinkers have applied free market assumptions in particular ways – especially as they relate to corporate governance. Hence, the purpose of the next chapter is not to demonstrate that these neoliberal ideas have influenced corporate governance but to think through how corporate governance – as a particular form of knowledge – has come to support a particular processes of corporate restructuring that contrasts with neoliberalism. Before that, however, I want to finish this chapter by looking at the concentration of financial assets in order to illustrate how monopoly has become embedded in a political-economic project which enrols a broader cross-section of society than admitted by the critical scholars I mentioned at the start of the chapter.

This all starts with a look at how financialization has spread throughout society. One key aspect of the financialization process

Chapter 3. Corporate Monopoly and its Neoliberal Cheerleaders

discussed above is the increasing dominance of large financial institutions in the control and ownership of corporations through share ownership. The financialization of public equity markets (i.e. shareholding) is tied into the specific forms of corporate governance I'll discuss in the next chapter. As illustrated in Figure 3.1 at the start of this chapter, however, the expansion of public equity markets in the Atlantic Heartland economies has been accompanied by a significant rise in inequality as the top 1% has increased their share of national income and wealth. This has been identified as a key example of why financialization is part of a neoliberal project to restore class power by the likes of Harvey, Dumenil and Levy, and others (see above). What it misses, however, is the concentration of financial assets and what these might mean, especially as they relate to the emergence of institutional investors (e.g. pension, insurance and mutual funds).[42] Again, I'll come back to some of this in the next chapter, but for now it is useful to highlight the major expansion of financial assets over the course of the last four to five decades.

This growth of financial assets has primarily resulted from the expansion of institutional investment funds. Before the GFC, the wealth of institutional investors represented a significant proportion of GDP in countries like the USA, UK and Canada, especially pension funds. For example, according to Ismael Erturk and colleagues the assets held by these institutional investors represented nearly 246% of US GDP in 2005 and nearly 214% of UK GDP, compared with a world average of 100% GDP.[43] Dissecting these figures reveals that a significant proportion of this investment is pension funds (121% and 73% respectively), which contrasts sharply with countries like France, Japan and Germany. A more detailed look at the history of institutional investment in the UK shows that such pension funds emerged as important financial players in the pre-neoliberal era – if we accept the idea that there has been a neoliberal age at all. Between 1957 and 1981, for example, these institutional funds increased 19-fold, reaching 62% of UK GDP in 1981; however, pension funds outstripped mutual and insurance funds in this period rising 30-fold.[44] While most of these pension funds started out as defined-benefit schemes, they are now mostly defined-contribution schemes invested in stock markets – hence why the UK equity market has rising so sharply since 1980 (see Figure 3.5).

These figures show the real expansion of financial assets over the last few decades, the benefits of which do not simply go to the top 1%. In fact, recent work by Gerald Davis shows that financial concentration involves the concentration of financial assets in the hands of institutional investment funds, especially in the US where indirect ownership of the stock market through such funds took off in 1977.[45] What Davis illustrates in his work is that there has been a reversal in shareholding from individuals to institutional investors. The percentage of Fortune 1000 corporations owned by these institutions rose from 35% in 1980 to 72% in 2005, for example, while the amount under management rose from $134 billion to $10 trillion in the same period (pp.15-16). What is most interesting about this dominance by institutional investors is that the three largest investors (Fidelity, Vanguard and American Funds) own a third of these funds. Now, what is important to understand here are the limitations that this concentration places on the operation of these funds and how it generates systemic inter-dependencies like those that caused the GFC. First, a rising proportion of shares of publicly-traded corporations are owned by these funds, meaning the funds are invested in companies that cannot effectively compete with each other because then the investor would end up competing with themselves. Second, any attempt by the funds to divest themselves of the shares could have a major impact on the share price, driving it down before all the shares can be sold and thereby leading to losses for the fund if it sought to divest. What Gerald Davis concludes is that the rise of these institutional

Chapter 3. Corporate Monopoly and its Neoliberal Cheerleaders

investors has led to "a surprising combination of concentration and liquidity" (p.20), which necessitates the capacity to purchase and sell large portions of stock at short notice meaning that these investors are end up only interested in shareholder value maximization (see next chapter).

Conclusion

The point of the discussion above is to highlight the fact that financialization involves more than the top 1%. Institutional investors represent the money of 'Joe and Jane Public' invested in their pensions, savings accounts, insurance funds, and so on. It is not just the top echelons of society who are invested (socially, politically, personally) in the financialized transformation of society. I've not even mentioned the investment people make in housing; I'll come back to this in Chapters 4 and 5. Alongside the investment in financial assets, this could form part of a broader story of our economies structural transformation into neoliberal-financial capitalism, but it cannot be left as a simple tale of the restoration of the top 1%. What has happened in the US, UK and Canada has necessitated the enrolment of broad swathes of society; the working and middle classes are tied into the extension of home ownership, pensions and other financial assets. We are all complicit in the financialization of the economy, whether or not we have been directly responsible for the imposition of particular ideas, policies or other activities. If we ignore this and focus on class power, we miss the important politics of these changes that Thomas Frank highlights in his book, *What's Wrong with Kansas?*[46]

Now, one thing the global financial crisis (GFC) has done is highlight corporate monopoly and this concentration of assets and wealth in our societies. While we may have a knee-jerk and negative reaction to monopoly, it's as important to understand how the concentration of income, wealth, assets and so forth helped to create the systemic conditions in which problems with one part of the economy rolled out across the rest of the economy. So when we talk about businesses being too-big-to-fail (TBTF), what we are really talking about is the systemic inter-dependencies that engender and reinforce instability. In this sense, we cannot simply let banks or other financial companies fail without suffering significant consequences elsewhere – our pensions depend on these companies, as do our jobs and the value of our assets. The ongoing merging and amalgamation of businesses into larger and larger organizations has only exacerbated this problem; it has not, as neoliberal thinkers contend, led to greater efficiencies or more consumer welfare. The reverse is probably true, in fact, once we calculate the total costs of the GFC. The dominance of corporate monopolies and the concentration of financial assets in the hands of a few massive institutional investors have contributed to the systemic instabilities that led to the GFC, and which we continue to face.

While I want to highlight the problems brought about by this re-emergence of corporate monopoly and the concentration of financial assets, I don't want to fall into the trap of assuming that this is some sort of structural project undertaken with the interests of the top 1% foremost in mind. Even if it is an unconscious plan, or some structural logic, understanding what has been happening over the last few years requires us to acknowledge the complexity of our own roles in creating this crisis and its consequences. The sociologist Susanne Soderbergh, for example, has called this "cannibalistic capitalism" because it has involved exploiting ourselves (e.g. wage restraint) at one end of the economy spectrum in order to benefit at the other end (e.g. pensions, housing).[47] To me, this is a more useful way to characterize much of what has happened. We have ended up cannibalizing ourselves, metaphorically and economically. Thus it's not the banks that are zombies, or the neoliberal ideas that did so much to legitimate finance, or even neoliberalism itself, as so many commentators contend; we are the zombies, chowing down

Chapter 3. Corporate Monopoly and its Neoliberal Cheerleaders

on our own brains and those of our neighbours with wanton disregard for the consequences of our actions or the indigestion we'll suffer.

1   Relevant literature from the critical perspective include: Harvey, D. (2005) *A Brief History of Neoliberalism*. Oxford: Oxford University Press; Harvey, D. (2010) *The Enigma of Capital and the Crises of Capitalism*. Profile Books; Duménil, G. and Lévy, D. (2004) *Capital Resurgent*. Cambridge, MA: Harvard University Press; Duménil, G. and Lévy, D. (2011) *The Crisis of Neoliberalism*. Cambridge, MA: Harvard University Press; and, Peet, R. (2007) *The Geography of Power*. London: Zed Books.
2   A good starting point for an interest reader in these critical perspectives might be a couple of articles by the geographer Simon Springer: e.g., Springer, S. (2010) Neoliberalism and geography: expansions, variegations, formations. *Geography Compass* 4(8): 1025-1038; and, Springer, S. 2012. Neoliberalism as discourse: between Foucauldian political economy and Marxian poststructuralism. *Critical Discourse Studies* 9(2): 133-147.
3   Duménil and Lévy, *The Crisis of Neoliberalism*, note 1.
4   Harvey, *A Brief History of Neoliberal*ism, note 1.
5   Van Apeldoorn, B. and Overbeek, H. (eds) (2012) *Neoliberalism in Crisis*. Basingstoke: Palgrave Macmillan, p.5.
6   Phelan, S. (2007) Review Essay: Messy grand narrative or analytical blind spot? When speaking of neoliberalism. *Comparative European Politics* 5(3): 328-338.
7   Dicken, P. (2011) *Global Shift*. New York: Guildford Press.
8   A few examples include: Krippner, G. (2005) The financialization of the American economy. *Socio-Economic Review* 3: 173-208; Palley, T. (2007) *Financialization: What It Is and Why It Matters*. Levy Economics Institute: Economics Working Paper Archive Working Paper 525; Pike, A., and Pollard, J.

(2010) Economic Geographies of Financialization. *Economic Geography* 86(1): 29-51; and, Birch, K. and Mykhnenko, V. (in press) Lisbonizing vs. financializing Europe? The Lisbon Strategy and the (un-)making of the European knowledge-based economy. *Environment and Planning C*.
9 Harvey, *A Brief History of Neoliberalism*, note 1, pp.161-2.
10 Harvey, *The Enigma of Capital*, note 1, p.245.
11 Duménil and Lévy, *The Crisis of Neoliberalism*, note 1, pp.17-18, 35.
12 Hager, S.B. (2012) Investment Bank Power and Neoliberal Regulation: From the Volcker Shock to the Volcker Rule, in H. Overbeek and B. van Apeldoorn (eds) *Neoliberalism in Crisis*. Basingstoke: Palgrave Macmillan, pp. 68-92.
13 Available online: http://topincomes.g-mond.parisschoolofeconomics.eu/
14 Helleiner, E. (1994) *States and the Reemergence of Global Finance: From Bretton Woods to the 1990s*. Ithaca: Cornell University Press.
15 Panitch, L. and Konings, M. (2009) Myths of Neoliberal Deregulation. *New Left Review* 57: 67-83.
16 The Policy Tensor blog, *The Eurodollar Market* (25 April 2013), available online: http://policytensor.com/2013/04/25/ the-eurodollar-market/
17 See Davies, A. (2012) *The Evolution of British Monetarism: 1968-1979*. University of Oxford: Discussion Papers in Economic and Social History Number 104.
18 Policy Tensor, *The Eurodollar Market*, note 16.
19 Data adapted from Philbeam, K. (2013) *International Finance* (4th Edition). Basingstoke: Palgrave Macmillan, available online: http://www.palgrave.com/business/pilbeam_int/ students/intros/12.htm
20 Varoufakis, Y. (2011) *Global Minotaur*. London: Zed Books.
21 One example of this is the idea that corporations now outnumber countries in the top 100 economies of the world;

for example, Hertz, N. (2002) *The Silent Takeover.* London: Arrow.
22   Vitali, S., Glattfelder, J. and Battiston, S. (2011) The network of global corporate control. *PLoS ONE* 6(1): e25995.
23   Baran, P. and Sweezy, P. (1966) *Monopoly Capital.* New York: Monthly Review Press. There are other examples of monopolies going back to the 1940s as shown by Harland Prechel (2000) *Big Business and the State.* Albany: State University of New York Press. According to a table in Prechel's book (p.82), industries as disparate as "Industrial trucks and tractors" (57% market share) and "Sewing machines" (78%) were dominated by the four largest four companies in 1947.
24   Foster, J.B., McChesney, R. and Jonna, R.J. (2011) Monopoly and Competition in Twenty-first Century Capitalism. *Monthly Review* 62(11), available online: http://monthlyreview.org/2011/04/01/monopoly-and-competition-in-twenty-first-century-capitalism
25   Klein, N. (2007) *Shock Doctrine.* Toronto: Vintage Canada, p.17.
26   Dicken, *Global Shift,* note 7.
27   Fishman, C. (2006) *The Wal-Mart Effect.* London: Penguin Books.
28   *The Economist* (3 Nov 2012), available online: http://www.economist.com/news/finance-and-economics/21565609-economies-scale-run-out-certain-point-largest-firms-america-may-be
29   Lynn, B. (2010) *Cornered.* New Jersey: John Wiley & Sons.
30   Lynn, B. (2005) *End of the Line.* New York: Doubleday.
31   Roy, (1997) *Socializing Capital: The Rise of the Large Industrial Corporation in America.* Connecticut: Princeton University Press.
32   Quoted in Greider, W. (1987) *Secrets of the Temple: How the Federal Reserve Runs the Country.* Simon & Schuster, p.93.
33   Crouch, C. (2011) *The Strange Non-Death of Neoliberalism.*

Cambridge: Polity, see Chapter 3.

34 It is possible that this "neoliberal" perspective is actually much older if we accept Karl Polanyi's argument that 'free' markets always had to be 'instituted' (i.e. planned, introduced and maintained by the state); if we agree with Polanyi on this front, however, we have to acknowledge that there is then very little to distinguish nineteenth century liberalism from twentieth century neo-liberalism – they seem virtually the same (hence, again, why we might say that we have never been neoliberal); see, Polanyi, K. (1944[2001]) *The Great Transformation*. Boston: Beacon Press.

35 Crouch, *The Strange Non-death of Neoliberalism*, note 33, pp.55-6.

36 Davies, W. (2010) Economics and the 'nonsense' of law: The case of the Chicago antitrust revolution. *Economy and Society* 39(1), pp.71-2

37 For example, Jensen, M. and Meckling, W. (1976) Theory of the firm: Managerial behavior, agency costs and ownership structure. *Journal of Financial Economies* 3: 305-360.

38 Madrick, J. (2011) *Age of Greed*. Toronto: Knopf, pp.82-3.

39 Crouch, *The Strange Non-death of Neoliberalism*, note 33, p.56.

40 Data available online: Samuel H. Williamson, 'S&P Index, Yield and Accumulated Index, 1871 to Present,' MeasuringWorth, 2012, http://www.measuringworth.com/datasets/sap/; and, http://www.finfacts.com/Private/curency/ftseperformance.htm

41 Wilks, S. (2013) *The Political Power of the Business Corporation*. Basingstoke: Edward Elgar.

42 See Cumbers, A. (2013) *Reclaiming Public Ownership*. London: Zed Books.

43 Erturk, I., Froud, J., Johal, S., Leaver, A. and Williams, K. (eds) (2008) *Financialization at Work: Key Texts and Commentary*. London: Routledge, p.5

44 Data comes from Coakley, J. and Harris, L. (1983) *City of*

Capital. Oxford: Blackwell, pp.95-6.
45 Davis, G. (2008) A new finance capitalism? Mutual funds and ownership re-concentration in the United States. *European Management Review* 5(1): 11-21.
46 Franks, T. (2004) *What is Wrong With Kansas?* Henry Holt and Co.
47 Soederberg, S. (2010) Cannibalistic Capitalism: The Paradoxes of Neoliberal Pension Securitization, in L. Panitch, G. Albo and V. Chibber (eds.) *Socialist Register 2011: The Crisis this Time*. London: Merlin Press.

Chapter 4

Assetization and the Concentration of Economic Power

Introduction

The last chapter should have shown you that when politicians, policy-makers, businesspeople and academics talk about *free* markets, they don't mean what they say or, if they do, then they have been seriously tucking into the Kool-Aid. What is perhaps more worrying, however, is that we, as public citizens and crown subjects, have also come to buy into the dominant discourse we hear daily on the radio and television and read about in the newspapers. Our lives are now intricately bound up with the exploitation of ourselves, our friends and family, our colleagues and so on. Although the "zombie-neoliberalism" trope has perhaps been overplayed somewhat, it does provide an apt metaphor for our self-cannibalism, or what we could think of as *auto-neoliberal-zombification*. My intention is not to get into that in this chapter, however.

What I'm intending to do instead is consider yet another critical take on neoliberalism, this time the idea that it is better understood as a process rather than a set of specific conditions, policies or outcomes. The reason for doing this is that I think this critical perspective misses two important things, as I'll highlight in a few pages time. Briefly here, the idea that neoliberalism is a process leaves us with a gap as to who is responsible for the invention and implementation of market-based mechanisms, instruments and incentives. As I also point out below, what these critics also miss is that many of these things are not in fact market-based at all since neoliberalism plays second fiddle to the re-emergence of corporate monopolies which inhibit the operation of markets, at least according to economic assump-

Chapter 4. Assetization and the Concentration of Economic Power

tions. Whether or not we accept that monopolies are bad for the *proper* functioning of markets is really beside the point, however; we simply have to acknowledge that large, monopolistic businesses are powerful social agents that influence how we want our societies and economies to be organized.[1] Again, whether this influence has negative or positive effects is beside the point. What matters is that we are supposed to be living in democratic societies where the decisions of the populace determine the various policies we end up living under. If we lose power over our lives, we lose power whether or not someone else is making benign or malign choices.

Now, this raises a serious question about who we should target as responsible for all the negative things we face today – uncertainty, unemployment, rising personal debt, reduced social mobility, etc., etc. If we accept that neoliberalism is a process, we end up with a disparate, diffuse target – it could, quite literally, be anyone. It is for this primary reason that I want to rethink our characterization of the last half-century. My view is that we can identify a better target by thinking about other ways to criticize this transformation, especially the shift from wage-based economies to asset-based economies, or what I'm calling a process of *assetization*. In this chapter, I focus especially on the changes that have happened to corporate governance over this period of time because I want to highlight possible targets for activism, protest and dissent. This should then provide the springboard for my 'manifesto' in Chapter 5.

What is Neoliberalism IV: A Process of Neoliberal Restructuring?

This chapter brings me to the final set of critical perspectives, mostly drawn from the discipline of human geography. A number of geographers have criticized the idea that neoliberalism can be characterized as either a singular and homogenous condition or singular and homogenous set of outcomes – that is, that neoliberalism is *one* force making us do the same things and leading to the same effects wherever we are in the world. These scholars are probably best exemplified by Jamie Peck and Adam Tickell, but include others as well.[2] What they all emphasize is the need to understand neoliberalism as a process, or *neoliberalization* in their terms – that is, a process of neoliberal restructuring.

The process of neoliberalization involves what Tickell and Peck call the *"mobilization of state power in the contradictory extension and reproduction of market(-like) rule"*.[3] In these terms neoliberalism is more than deregulation, privatization, liberalization or any of the other constituent elements I outlined in the book's introduction. Instead it is the blurring of the distinction between market and state, in which the state plays an active role. This means that the state is not hollowed out since public spending cuts, budgetary constraints, austerity policies, monetary price stability, etc. are all tied into the (contradictory) extension of the state's role as enabler and promoter of markets. The state enables the transfer of spending from one area (e.g. industrial policy) to another (e.g. debt interest), the transformation of state's role from one thing to another (e.g. from welfare to workfare), and so on.

One very helpful thing that Tickell and Peck do is periodize neoliberalism, identifying three different phases, which they call: "proto-neoliberalism", "roll-back neoliberalism" and "roll-out neoliberalism" (see Figure 4.1). These different periods correspond to specific characteristics of neoliberalism at different points in its evolution – the significance of this is obvious when we think back to Chapter 1 and the evolution of neoliberal thinking. What these phases illustrate is that neoliberalism is not *one* thing, *one* policy, *one* regime, and forth. For example, the intellectual project of Hayek, Friedman and the like was replaced by more specific state projects pursued by Ronald Reagan, Margaret Thatcher and Brian Mulroney as neoliberal ideas led to the 'roll-back' of Keynesianism; this was then superseded by the 'roll-out' of market institutions in an attempt to resolve the negative consequences (e.g. unemployment) of the earlier phase of neoliberalism. This last phase is characteristic of centre-left governments in the 1990s, especially those of President Bill Clinton and Prime Minister Tony Blair, providing support for the important argument that neoliberalism does not equal conservatism.

FIGURE 4.1: Phases of Neoliberalism

	PROTO	ROLL-BACK	ROLL-OUT
When	Pre-1980	1980s to early 1990s	Early 1990s to financial crisis
Discourse	Anti-Keynesian	Deregulation, small state	Paternal state
Intellectual frontier	Monetarist economics	Supply-side economics	Bourgeois sociology
Key figures	Friedman, Hayek, Pinochet	Thatcher, Reagan	Clinton, Blair, Schroder, Greenspan
Service delivery	Spending cuts	Privatization	Marketization
Fiscal position	Stagflation	Tight money, loose credit	Deflation
Heartland	Chicago	London, Washington DC	Brussels, London, Washington DC
Fiscal discipline	Inflation	Structural adjustment	Standards and codes
Ethics	Individualism	Amoral marketization	Moral authoritarianism

Source: Tickell, A. and Peck, J. (2003) Making global rules: globalisation or neoliberalization, in J. Peck and H. Yeung (eds) *Remaking the global economy.* London: Sage, pp.163-182.

What these critics highlight is the need to go beyond simplistic assumptions about what neoliberalism *does* when it *happens* to a country or society. What they are interested in is the active participation of specific actors, whether these are national, local or municipal politicians and policy-makers, private sector businesses, third sector organizations and so on. As Peck and Tickell explain, neoliberalization entails "necessarily variegated and uneven" effects.[4] It is hybrid, geographically specific and contextual – consequently it makes little sense to talk about neoliberalism everywhere around the world in singular or similar terms. This argument is born out in a range of research that has identified very different and distinctive *varieties of neoliberalism*, including my own work as well as many other, far more insightful writers.[5]

Like the other critical perspectives I've mentioned already in this book, however, it's also possible to take issue with this particular perspective. First, the idea that neoliberalism is a process means we lose any concrete sense of *who* is responsible for the implementation of market-based mechanisms, instruments and incentives. By definition, as a process neoliberalization involves hybrid, heterogeneous, uneven, etc. responsibilities for these things – in one case it might be city officials, in another global business elites, in another do-gooder conservationists, and so on. Consequently there is no target for our ire, or at least no easy target for our ire, which might explain why popular movements have recently focused on the top 1% – whether the top 1% are symbolic or concrete is beside the point, at least they're a target we can all identify. Second, this perspective does not really address the issues I've highlighted in the last few chapters, namely the rise and role of corporations and corporate actors in the expansion of 'neoliberalism'. In focusing on corporations as organizational actors I'm able to analyze the *meso-level* – to use an horrific piece of social science jargon – or organizational scale. So, rather than making broad claims about society (macro) or specific claims about individuals

Chapter 4. Assetization and the Concentration of Economic Power

(micro), my argument is that we can identify key organizations and their impacts on society without losing sight of what is responsible (e.g. corporations) or succumbing to the idea of our helplessness in the face of overwhelming odds. As mentioned in the Introduction, Geoffrey Hodgson points out that most economic activity happens within economic organizations and especially within corporations of one sort or another.[6] It therefore seems necessary to focus our attention at this political-economic level if we want to understand where we've come from and where we're heading.

With the concept of neoliberalization, in contrast, we are left with a rather *macro* view of our societies which does not explore the specifics of the meso-level (or organizational) changes that we have and are going through. I think that the key framing of neoliberalization as the *"extension and reproduction of market(-like) rule"* – as outlined by Tickell and Peck – kind of misses the point. It is not market-like rule we have seen emerge over the last 30-40 years, it is the opposite, or *monopoly-like rule* – this is even admitted by neoliberal thinkers themselves as they have sort to legitimate monopoly (see last chapter). These gaps have led me to think about ways we might otherwise characterize the transformation of our economies, one of which is the notion of *assetization* which I think better reflects all the changes I've highlighted so far and those I'll discuss now.

Assetization: The Dynamics, Logics and Governance of Assets

Obviously I want to start by outlining what I mean by *assetization*. As a reader you might start by asking why we need yet another long-winded word to describe the changes to our economies over the last four decades. Well, I don't think that neoliberalization (or financialization for that matter) captures everything that's going on, and nor do I think it's an adequate explanations for a whole series of changes set in motion *before* the

1980s. For example, within critical accounts of neoliberalism there are numerous references to *commodification* as a key example of a market-based process – that is, the transformation of objects, relations, interactions, etc. into things for sale. There is little doubt that this is happening, what is missing from this account, however, is the transformation of things into assets – that is, resources that generate income without the necessity of sale (see below). This is what assetization refers to. More broadly, it is the gradual shift from:

- Economies dependent on commodity production, wage-income and forms of mass consumption financed by workers' wages;
to ...
- Economies dependent on asset creation, asset-income and forms of consumption financed by rising asset values and new debt instruments.

If we want to understand this we have to understand assets, especially how they are accounted for, identified and defined at the organizational level. Here we need to turn to accountancy, which is a fascinating profession – no really it is! According to the *International Accounting Standards,* an asset is defined as:

> "...a resource that is controlled by the entity as a result of past events (for example, purchase or self-creation) and from which future economic benefits (inflows of cash or other assets) are expected. [IAS 38.8]"[7]

Assets are property (i.e. they are controlled) and resources (i.e. they produce income) at the same time; unlike commodities. Back at the start of the twentieth century, Thorstein Veblen defined assets as "capitalized on the basis of income-yielding capacity, and possibly vendible under the cover of a corporation security

Chapter 4. Assetization and the Concentration of Economic Power

(as, e.g., common stock), or even under the usual form of private sale". Moreover, Veblen states that "capitalization ... is a special case of valuation" which has important implications for understanding how our economies have changed.[8]

What makes this so important now is that assets provide an income; they are not just a commodity which can be exchanged for money from customers. Commodities are produced explicitly for market exchange and have a specific logic as a consequence; that is, commodities are subject to supply and demand dynamics in which demand leads to increasing supply and therefore falling prices (if we assume 'normal' market functioning) subject to (income) inflation.[9] An asset, on the other hand, entails a wholly different logic; demand for an asset does not lead to falling prices but instead makes the asset more valuable leading to asset price inflation (the 'good' sort of inflation). In this sense, market competition – which neoliberals bang on about incessantly – loses its relevance for asset-holders and producers since demand drives up the value of their assets no matter what and no matter whether they are competitors or not. It is the people buying assets who end up competing, which is akin to customers competing with each other for commodities and not the producers competing with each other for customers.

Why might this happen? Well, it is often difficult, if not impossible, to increase the supply of assets. Take a music CD or film DVD for example; these are products sold as commodities to consumers that go up or down in price depending on demand – hence why popular music and films are cheaper than niche ones. Behind this music and cinema, however, are a series of intellectual property rights (IPRs) that reserve the copyright of the music or film to the holder of the copyright and no one else. This copyright is an asset; it is a resource that can be used to make CDs or DVDs as well as producing licensing income from the sale of those products. However, because there is only one copyright holder, demand for that copyright is not subject to the same supply and demand dynamics. If the particular music or film becomes more popular, then the value of the copyright will increase because the licensing income will increase. All this has made IPRs more valuable and hence explains the concerted efforts made by MNCs – especially from the USA – to incorporate intellectual property rights into the World Trade Organization.[10]

The above example should not imply that assets, like other resources, are 'natural' or 'inherent'; instead it is meant to show that they are constructed through private and public decisions like the establishment of IP rules. Copyright, for example, is not valuable unless there is a legal system to establish it and then prosecute people who break copyright (e.g. Napster in the early 2000s). Moreover, assets are often only valuable because there cost can be capitalized over a period of time (e.g. housing mortgages). This temporal side of assets is important because it helps to explain how asset values can increase significantly over a period of time (e.g. how a house can double in price over a decade). It would be almost impossible to construct demand for assets if we had to pay the full price at purchase rather than defray the cost through some form of capitalization (e.g. mortgage). Consequently, a secondary logic underpinning assets is the potential, even expectation, of capital gains (i.e. asset price inflation); this sits alongside any 'income-yielding capacity' identified by Veblen (see above). More recently, and through the introduction of new accounting practices like fair value accounting (FVA), large corporations have been able to book this capital gains as profit – while any capital fall has to be booked as a loss.[11] The primary effect of this is that any upward or downward movement in asset value has a dramatic impact on corporate profits and the continuation of the business as a going concern. In his recent book, *Material Markets*, Donald MacKenzie provides a good introduction to this sort of measurement and accounting practice and its impacts – one of the main ones being the collapse of Enron, Worldcom, Tyco, and so on in the early

2000s.[12]

Macro-view: The Emergence of Asset-based Economies

Having discussed what makes assets unique and why assetization is an important process, I now want to run through the specifics of assetization at different levels of society. I'll begin with the macro-level (societal) then continue with the micro-level (individual) before finishing with the meso-level (organizational) – the last of these is the scale I want to focus on in this chapter. The macro-level of assetization is exemplified by two key societal trends: first, the differential share of national income that accrues to financial asset owners (or *rentiers* – see Box 4.1) rising at the expense of wage earners; and, second, the rising value of assets across asset classes, especially housing. What is the evidence for these claims?

Box 4.1 Rent-seeking and the *Rentier*

In the later nineteenth and early twentieth centuries there was a growing concern in capitalist countries, especially Britain, that a certain type of capitalist were benefiting from the growth of financial markets, and at the expense of other capitalists into the bargain. People like R.H. Tawney (1921) and John Maynard Keynes (1936) criticized the growth of these "passive" capitalists who were more concerned with the income they gained from their assets than with responsibly managing or monitoring those assets. They called this type of capitalist *rentiers* because they were more concerned with rent-seeking income (e.g. interest payments, share dividends) than productive wealth generation (e.g. investment). Rentiers engage in precisely those speculative activities we now associate

---

> with banks and other financial institutions, and are only concerned with ensuring that their assets are as liquid as possible so that they can sell them at a moment's notice.
>
> **Source:** R.H. Tawney (1921) *The Acquisitive Society*. London: G. Bell & Sons Ltd.; John Maynard Keynes (1936) *The General Theory of Interest, Employment and Money*. London: Macmillan.

1. According to a 2011 academic article by Christoph Deutschman, the share of national income going to financial asset owners "went up in most OECD countries, first between the 1960s and 1970s, and even more after 1980".[13] At the same time the share of national income going to wage earners fell. Other scholars like Greta Krippner and Thomas Palley have made similar claims about these changes, especially about the expansion of the financial sector as a key sector in the economy resulting from rising lending (see previous chapters).[14] What this means is that there has been a significant increase in levels of debt across the Atlantic heartland *and* a consequent increase in interest payments on this debt, both of which have replaced employment and wages as the key policy and political concern (as mentioned in Chapter 2) – rising household debt is show in Figure 4.2.

Chapter 4. Assetization and the Concentration of Economic Power

FIGURE 4.2: Total Credit to Households (& Non-profit Institutions Serving Households) in USA, UK and Canada (%GDP)

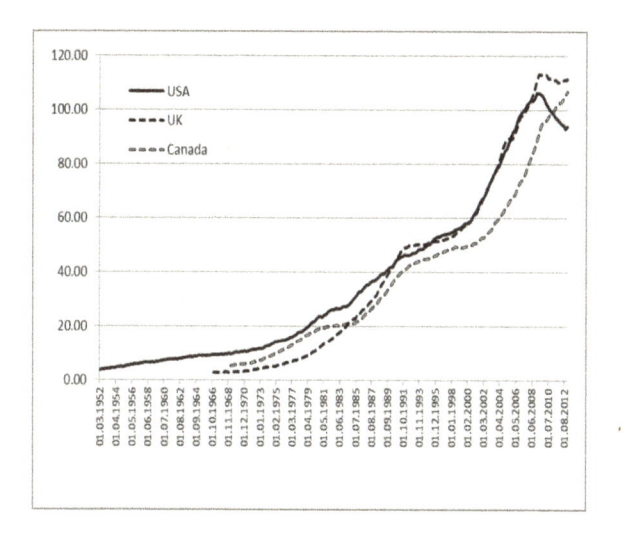

Source: Bank of International Settlements (debt) and OECD, National Accounts (GDP).[15]

2. According to house price trends, the real value of housing assets has increased significantly since the 1970s with particular spikes in house prices in the late 1970s, late 1980s and then during the 2000s until the GFC brought it all to a crashing halt. What we tend to forget is that these house price rises are dependent on mortgages (i.e. bank lending), which are financial assets held by banks, and that it is house price *rises* that contribute to home-owners wealth – rising house prices and annual house price rises in the UK are shown in Figure 4.3. This form of "asset price Keynesianism" is discussed at some length by Robert Brenner in a 2009 paper about the US economy and its dependence on household debt financed by home equity withdrawals, rising house values, etc.[16]

FIGURE 4.3: Average UK House Price (left) and Average House Annual Price Change (right) (1952-2010)

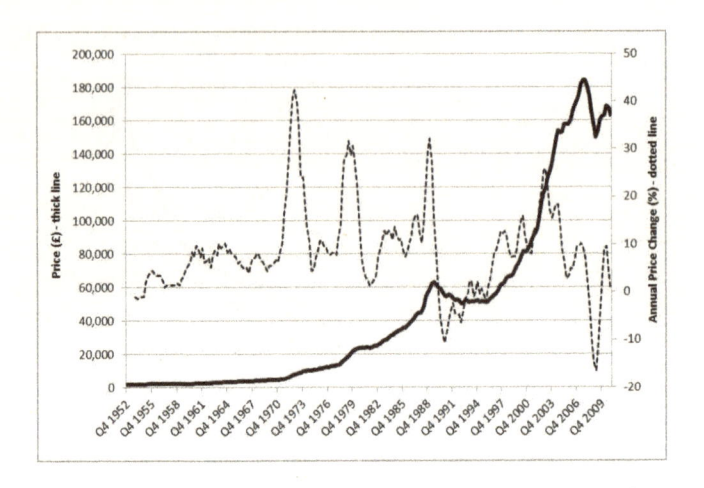

Source: UK House Prices Since 1952, Nationwide Building Society.[17]

As usual, I'm not the first to notice these societal trends. Others have written about them and are writing about it now. One example is a 2010 paper in the journal *Housing Studies* by the political scientist Matthew Watson; he argues that the rise of home ownership enabled by rising household debt has created an "asset-holding society" in which "general credit expansion facilitates inflationary pressure on asset prices".[18] Inflation of asset prices is here promoted as a virtue even when it is condemned as a vice when related to wages (see Chapter 2 discussion of monetarism). A second example is the recent book *The Making of the Indebted Man* where the author, Maurizio Lazzarato, characterizes our societies as "debt economies".[19] By this he means that interest payments from loans of all sorts (e.g. mortgages, credit cards, student loans, public debt, corporate debt, etc.) have replaced other forms of income (e.g. wages) as the dominant source of income, profit and disciplinary mechanism (i.e.

Chapter 4. Assetization and the Concentration of Economic Power

controlling force of our behaviour). While Lazzarato writes about the implications of this transformation for individuals (which I will come back to below and in the next chapter), what he does not do is extend his arguments to their logical conclusion; we are not *just* part of a debt economy, we are also necessarily part of an asset economy. Those debts, whoever or whatever has incurred them, are also assets for someone or something else.

Now, debt, credit and assets are all deeply implicated in the GFC. In their recent book, Duménil and Lévy argue that the GFC resulted from the massive expansion of financial assets, especially loans, derivatives and securities, as well as over-the-counter (OTC) trades like the credit default swaps (CDSs).[20] The numbers we're talking about are truly astonishing, hard even to comprehend. We have to wrap our head around the fact that these financial assets represented between 450% and 700% of GDP for countries like the USA and UK (respectively).[21] What these figures imply is that debt (the corollary of assets) also increased to these astonishing levels, largely as the result of mass leveraging by banks against their asset base.[22] Borrowing increased across all sectors of the economy, whether corporate, household or government. Each sector increased their purchasing of assets and their borrowing to pay for them; this is evident in rising levels of corporate debt, public debt, and household debt throughout the Atlantic Heartland.[23] What enabled this expansion of debt were new financial instruments like securitization, public-private partnering, and home equity lines of credit (HELOC). More to the point, what this debt expansion enabled was the creation of new asset income streams, including second-order, third-order and fourth-order income streams:

First-order: asset itself and income from asset.
Second-order: interest payments from the lending.

Third-order: securitization of lending through mechanisms like collateralized debt obligations (CDOs).

Fourth-order: over-the-counter trades to insure securities through mechanisms like credit default swaps (CDSs).

While these four orders are implicated in the transformation of our economies, it is third- and fourth-order income streams that are most closely tied to the GFC. It is these income streams that enabled a total separation of reality (e.g. credit-worthiness) from finance (e.g. subprime mortgage). It's also these forms of borrowing and asset creation that have been done to death in other books on the GFC and so I don't want to go into them here – it'll have to suffice to point you, the reader, to several helpful books in the Introduction of this book.

Micro-level: Assetization and the Capitalization of Our Lives

Next I'm going to outline the micro-level of assetization. Thinking about this micro-level echoes – but is not based on – the assumptions about self-interested and rational individuals underpinning much neoliberal economics. What is increasingly evident in popular, political and scholarly discourse is that anything can be (and is) capitalized as an asset. One troubling trend amongst economists and their policy-maker acolytes is to refer to various social, environmental and personal qualities and characteristic as forms of 'capital'. This is why we hear terms like social capital, human capital, natural capital, knowledge capital, etc. What they represent are far more human and humane than these terms imply, however, including our friendships, our education, our experience, our environment, the knowledge in our heads, etc.

Although it may be distasteful and disturbing to think about these things as assets – i.e. as property and income streams – they are increasingly and actively constructed as such through

Chapter 4. Assetization and the Concentration of Economic Power

changes in regulation, property and policy. One example will suffice here; student loans. In the USA student loan debt has increased from about $90 billion in 1999 to $550 billion in 2011, or a massive 511% increase over that period.[24] As a consequence, student debt is an increasingly political issue in the Atlantic Heartland where they have led to protests in Quebec, England and elsewhere; they even provided a significant stimulus to the Occupy Wall Street movement.[25] Now, one key rationale and justification behind increasing the level of student loans – and the ultimate costs paid by students – is that higher education benefits students by contributing to their human capital. Hence, it is perfectly reasonable to expect students to pay for their higher education because it benefits them personally later in life – here education is being capitalized as an asset held by students. Recently, a secret report by the UK government revealed plans to sell off student loan debt and enable an increase in the interest charges applied to this debt – we'll have to wait and see whether this happens.[26] This is just one example of what Veblen calls the capitalization of "habits of life", or the capitalization of intangible assets ranging from personal taste (e.g. fashion), birth (e.g. birthday presents), loyalty (e.g. reputation), and so on.[27] This example is supposed to show how assetization is not simply about the expansion and extension of abstract financial assets; it has direct and immediate impacts on a range of people.

As mentioned then, more and more parts of our personal and individual lives are capitalized as assets, even if we don't or can't spot it right away. Examples include our leisure time (e.g. taste, fashion), our work lives (e.g. education, knowledge generation), and even our personal relationships (e.g. contacts, networks) through new social media like Facebook and Twitter. On the one hand, this capitalization of our lives beyond (paid) labour has been presented as an opportunity for wide-scale solidarity and organizing by some leftists, especially those thinkers working in the *autonomist* Marxist tradition. A number of these autonomists have come up with concepts like 'immaterial labour', 'cognitive capitalism' and 'biocapitalism' to describe the transformation of industrialized societies.[28] What autonomist writers like Yann Moulier Boutang argue is that intellect, cognition, affect, emotion, relationships, social interaction, etc. are all being converted into "tradable assets".[29] While this extends exploitation of (unpaid) labour into our personal lives, it also represents an opportunity for positive change because it means that our very lives, our relationships, our intellect, our bodies can become sites of resistance. Consequently, if we simply open up and share our lives, our thoughts, our emotions, etc. we can resist the extension of capital and create new spaces of production which are not subject to enclosure – one example these thinkers refer to is the open source software movement where the collective and free labour of hundreds or thousands of programmers can produce workable and freely exchanged goods (e.g. *Open Office*).

On the other hand, this capitalization of our lives has led other leftist thinkers to argue that financial capitalism is a form of violence since it involves the explicit, if often indirect, exploitation of our lives. The Italian autonomist thinker Christian Marazzi makes this claim in reference to the outright exploitation of sub-prime borrowers from the mid-2000s.[30] The rise in sub-prime lending was premised on the direct exploitation of marginalized groups in society, especially in the USA where poor, African-American communities were particularly targeted by predatory lenders. The egregious tactics of these lenders are spelled out in Matt Taibbi's book *Griftopia*, which should be required reading for anyone who wants to understand the GFC.[31] The sheer audacity and outright stupidity of many financial (and non-financial) businesses in the run-up to the 2007-08 crash is really difficult to stomach when reading Taibbi's account, especially the actions of Goldman Sachs, which he memorably describes thus: "The world's most powerful investment bank is a great vampire squid wrapped around the face of humanity, relentlessly jamming its blood funnel into anything that smells like money" (p.209). The actions of banks, governments and others after 2007-08 are rage-inducing, to say the least. Whereas there is very direct violence committed against sub-prime borrowers, what Marazzi argues is that value extracted from various forms of unpaid labour beyond the workplace extend capital relations into our personal lives in other violent ways. An example of this is Facebook where our activities on the website – our relationships, our likes, our sharing – can all be mined and monetized by the company as it sells the information to advertisers and marketers.

Meso-view: Corporate Governance and Asset Value Maximization

I'm now coming to the main point of this chapter. Assetization is central for understanding the meso-level; that is, organizational restructuring and governance. Assets are central to the corporate dimension of our economies because businesses are defined by their assets, as well as liabilities – moreover, corporations and other businesses are themselves assets to their investors. According to accounting and corporate finance a business' balance sheet consists of assets and liabilities – these two should equal each other (see Box 4.2). What assetization has involved is the rising dominance of asset-holder interests (i.e. shareholders, or rentiers – see Box 4.1 above) over all other interests (e.g. workers, suppliers, customers) when it comes to organizing and running corporations. This increasing dominance of asset-holders is hardly surprising given the fact that an increasing amount of economic activity takes place within firms – which are defined both by their assets and as assets – and not within markets.

> **Box 4.2 Assets and Liabilities - An Easy Intro to Corporate Accounting**
>
> The balance sheet of every business consists of assets and liabilities. The way these two things are characterized sometimes conflicts with our common-sense definition of these terms. Assets basically include all the assets a business uses to run their activities (e.g. cash owed to it, inventories, tangible assets like buildings, intangible assets like brands) and liabilities include all the money they borrowed to pay for these assets (e.g. debt, equity) and any retained earnings or cash in the bank. Retained earnings and cash in the bank are liabilities because they don't *belong* to the business, but to the business owners. When it comes to publicly-listed corporations these owners are shareholders whose shares entitle them to a dividend, or proportion of these earnings / cash.
>
> **Source:** Brealey, R., Myers, S., Marcus, A., Maynes, E. and Mitra, D. (2003) *Fundamentals of Corporate Finance*. Toronto: McGraw-Hill.

This dominance of asset-holder interests is known as *shareholder value maximization* (SVM). William Lazonick and Mary O'Sullivan have described SVM as an "ideology" that underpins corporate governance and the drive to ramp up share prices (see Chapter 3).[32] Although these two authors equate the emergence of SVM with the "Reaganite and Thatcherite revolutions" (p.14), its pedigree stretches back further than this to the work of financial economists like Michael Jensen, Eugene Fama and others.[33] These scholars argued that corporations are not 'real entities' but instead a 'nexus of contracts' in which the interests of share-

Chapter 4. Assetization and the Concentration of Economic Power

holders, as owners of (investment) capital (but not the firm itself), is paramount. According to Rakesh Khurana and Locke and Spender, this argument, known as *agency theory*, has come to dominant how corporate governance is taught in business schools and how it's implemented in the companies themselves.[34] A number of people have even equated agency theory with neoliberalism, which is probably an accurate description although whether it has ever been fully or properly implemented is the real question.[35] Before I address this question I want to examine how assetization is manifested in corporate governance; this involves looking at how intangible assets are used to legitimate SVM.

The Rise of Intangible Assets
In order to understand the how corporate governance has been reoriented around SVM it is first necessary to understand how the way businesses are valued has been transformed by changes in accounting practices, especially in the accounting of *intangible assets*. Since I've already defined assets above, a good starting point for the discussion here is to define intangible assets. According to *International Accounting Standards* (IAS) rule 38.8, an intangible asset is:

> "...non-monetary assets which are without physical substance and identifiable (either being separable or arising from contractual or other legal rights). Intangible assets meeting the relevant recognition criteria are initially measured at cost, subsequently measured at cost or using the revaluation model, and amortised on a systematic basis over their useful lives (unless the asset has an indefinite useful life, in which case it is not amortised)."[36]

Thus intangible assets are those assets that have no "physical substance" and can include things like software and data, intellectual property rights, brand value, human and organizational capital, and 'goodwill' – see the OECD report on *Knowledge-based Capital* for examples.[37] All of these things represent something of value to a business, both a resource and an income stream, and they have also involved a reworking of accounting practices over the last few decades as they have *become* increasingly important to businesses. How intangible assets have become important is a key issue in my view – a more in-depth analysis is provided by Jose Palma in his 2009 article in the *Cambridge Journal of Economics*.[38]

While it might seem pretty easy to accept that things like buildings, machinery, tools, computer equipment, and so on have value, it's sometimes harder to get our head around the idea that ephemeral things also have value. For example, a brand has value because it will lead to future benefits (e.g. income) as customers seek out specific branded goods over others – this is why Coca-Cola's brand is so valuable. What I want to highlight here is that these intangible assets have become more important since the 1970s to the extent that they are now far more valuable than any tangible asset. As the graph in Figure 4.4 shows, intangible assets now represent 80% of the value of the biggest businesses, a reversal from the 1970s when tangible assets represented 80% of this value. This change illustrates the importance of brands, research, innovation, etc. (i.e. knowledge) to businesses, in contrast to physical assets like buildings, machinery, etc. The rise of intangible assets has driven policy-making in many countries towards the notion of *knowledge economies* as a result – see Jose Palma for a discussion of this.

Chapter 4. Assetization and the Concentration of Economic Power

FIGURE 4.4: The Rise of Intangible Assets: Proportion of S&P 500 Market Value

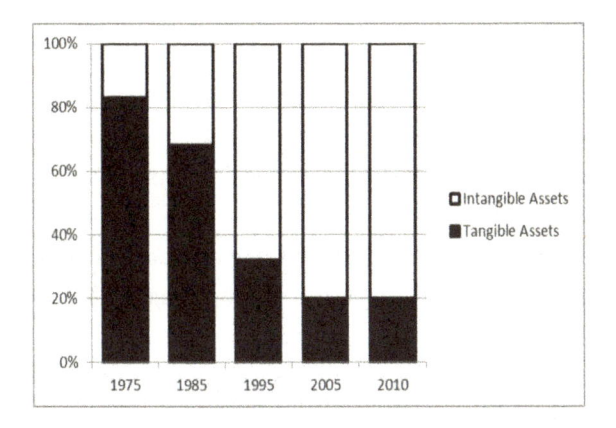

[Bar chart showing Intangible Assets vs Tangible Assets for years 1975, 1985, 1995, 2005, 2010. Tangible assets decrease from ~83% in 1975 to ~20% in 2010, while intangible assets increase correspondingly.]

Source: Adapted from Ocean Tomo LLC.[39]

Now, a lot has been written about the idea that developed economies like the US, UK and Canada are changing into 'knowledge-based economies' – according to one influential commentator, Charles Leadbeater, the argument goes like this:

> "Most of us make our money from thin air: we produce nothing that can be weighed, touched or easily measured. Our output is not stockpiled at harbours, stored in warehouses or shipped in railway cars."[40]

While it may seem odd to focus on something like knowledge and intangible assets in a book about neoliberalism, I do so because neoliberal ideas (if not policies or processes) are tied to this rise of intangible assets. One reason they are related is that corporate monopolies are enabled and reinforced by intangible assets as emerging intellectual property rights (IPRs) mean that such assets are now easier to enclose behind private property rights. These knowledge monopolies (e.g. patents, copyright, etc.) come to reinforce corporate (size) monopolies since they enable the capture of protected revenues (i.e. rent-seeking), which can be used to create or purchase new assets, restarting the cycle once again. At the meso-level then, intellectual and size monopolies are part and parcel of the expansion of asset values, one reinforces the other; size enables the creation and enforcement of intellectual assets, which provide revenues to grow bigger through the capture of new assets.

Intangible Assets, Corporate Restructuring and Corporate Governance
For me, the second and more interesting reason that intangible assets are related to corporate restructuring and governance, especially the growth of monopolies, is that they legitimate rising share prices under conditions specific to large, public corporations – that is, those businesses listed on public stock markets like the *New York Stock Exchange* (NYSE) and *London Stock Exchange* (LSE). The debate about the benefits of and problems with public corporations stretches back centuries – today it is usually reduced to an issue of corporate governance.[41] What this governance concerns is the question of how investors get their money back from their investment in a business. Businesses, in turn, use this investment to buy assets in order to create revenues to pay back investors. Here assetization is a double-sided concept in that businesses buy assets (e.g. machinery, buildings, brand value, etc.) while their equity counts as a financial asset (e.g. share) to investors. What complicates this relationship is the concentration of assets in one (monopolistic) organization – desired by business executives since monopolies ensure easy returns – and the dispersion of shares to create liquidity – desired by investors.[42] Connecting these different interests – the separation of control and ownership, as it is called – has been hotly debated throughout the twentieth century and now represents one of the key questions in corporate governance.

As mentioned in the last chapter, the last few years have been busy times for academics working in business schools as they tackle these corporate governance issues. Business scholars, frequently trained as economists, have promoted the idea that corporations and corporate monopolies are fine as long as they serve the interests of the shareholders, largely because they see shareholders as the 'owners' of corporations. The work of economists like Ronald Coase (see Chapter 3), Alchian and Demsetz, Jensen and Meckling, and Eugene Fama have all helped to promote the idea that SVM (i.e. the value of corporate assets) should trump any other corporate goal (e.g. public good).[43] However, SVM is, in turn, dependent on certain assumptions about markets being the most appropriate and efficient mechanism for working out the value of equity/shares – that is, value can only be determined from the result of people making exchanges on markets – see Box 4.3 for a discussion of this so-called "efficient market hypothesis". Hence, Colin Crouch points out that SVM and the assumptions about markets as *the* determinant of (asset) value involves a dangerous and self-reinforcing cycle that was built into corporate accounting:

"...even corporate accounting systems were changed, so that instead of estimating the values of the assets of a firm in terms of the value of its labour, capital, markets, etc., accountants looked simply at the stock market value of these assets, a value formed by traders' beliefs about other traders' beliefs, etc."[44]

Box 4.3 Efficient Market Hypothesis

The efficient market hypothesis (EMH) is the brainchild of Eugene Fama, a professor in Chicago's business school since the 1960s, who helped to found financial economics. The EMH is based on the idea that people are rational, self-interested individuals and that efficient markets reflect the underlying value of a business. This means that investors

> cannot out-perform other investors on the basis of existing and publicly available information. As the agents of owners, managers then have the responsibility to maximize this market value to the exclusion of all else. Along with the development of agency theory by the likes of Alchian and Demsetz and Jensen and Meckling, this hypothesis has led to the idea that the interests of managers and shareholders have to be aligned through executive share options and the like.
>
> **Source:** Rakesh Khurana (2007) *From Higher Aims to Hired Hands: The Social Transformation of American Business Schools and the Unfulfilled Promise of Management as a Profession*. Princeton: Princeton University Press, p.310.

Technically this means that asset values (or, really, shareholder value) are determined by the operations of traders making trades on the stock market; in this sense, there is no *underlying value* to any business' assets. This form of valuation is legitimated by the rise of intangible assets because anything that can't be accounted for after a market valuation (e.g. trading of shares) can be classed as part of the intangible assets of the business. Basically, and crudely, if the market capitalization of a corporation (i.e. its share value) cannot be accounted for by any physical and tangible assets, it can now be simply accounted for by something as ephemeral as 'goodwill' or human capital or branding.[45] This is how skyrocketing stock markets (see Figure 3.3 in the last chapter) have been legitimated – they are presented as the true reflection of market value. Meanwhile, corporate failures (e.g. bankruptcies) end up as major problems because the risk that an asset is not as valuable as it seems according to market signals is spread out amongst institutional investors who have bought into

Chapter 4. Assetization and the Concentration of Economic Power

the expectation of forever rising asset values legitimated by nothing more than the expectations and decisions of a bunch of traders.

This transformation of corporate organization and governance – driven by notions of market-determined value – is totally dependent on the rise of intangible assets and has significant implications for how corporations are managed and run, much of which relates back to my concern in the last chapter with the emergence of businesses – especially banks – that are too-big-to-fail. What has happened is that corporations have been turned into assets whose value needs to keep rising forever; this is because their share value represents the assets of institutional investors who are dependent on these rising asset values to ensure returns for their constituents (e.g. pensioners, savers, insurees, etc.). All this, however, has been underpinned by assumptions about rational self-interest on the part of *individual* human actors, rather than the consequences of the emergent properties of *inter-subjective* expectations. Basically, if we think everyone only thinks about their own self-interest, we forget that they might base their actions on what other people are doing. This is where we hit the real problem with our asset-based economies; as Mark Blyth points out the assumption that we only need to be concerned with micro-scale decisions (e.g. self-interest) simply ignores the fact that all these decisions lead to meso-level and macro-level effects that are more than the sum of their parts.[46] And, more importantly, since these meso and macro effects are systemic as well they can be highly destabilizing.

Despite these changes to corporate governance there is evidence that agency theory has been misapplied, or, more likely, that it was never applicable in the first place. Even Michael Jensen, doyen of agency theory, has claimed that agency theory has not been implemented properly or adequately (whether it can is another question), leading to significant and damaging consequences. This is spelled out by Dobbin and Jung in their contribution to the collected volume *Markets on Trial*.[47] What they argue is that institutional investors and financial analysts have been the prime drivers behind the adoption of this new form of corporate governance (i.e. SVM), which they adopted largely because the changes promised higher returns for investors and analysts. However, agency theory was actually "misapplied" according to Dobbin and Jung since it failed to align the interests of shareholders with executives despite the massive expansion of executive share options (p.37). What they show is that institutional investors now control 60% of shares in an average US corporation – up from 20% in 1970 – while "boards did not tie executives rewards to the long-term interests of shareholders" (p.38). What has resulted is a short-term focus on rising (and raising) share value, primarily through the management of revenues – basically, using various accounting practices to massage earnings. This necessitates keeping analysts on-board, leading to de-diversified – because they are easier to assess – and concentrated businesses – because monopolies have higher earnings power. In conclusion, Dobbin and Jung suggest that agency theory was misapplied, focused too much on short-term gains and therefore encouraging longer-term risks. Corporate governance was not, in this sense, part of a neoliberalization process, but rather a reflection of the concerns of economic actors who ramped up the value of corporate and financial assets at the expense of everything else.

Conclusion

What this chapter has focused on is neoliberalism as a process – that is, neoliberalization. This perspective is derived from the work of academics like Jamie Peck, Adam Tickell and others. They emphasize that neoliberalism is not a singular or homogenous set of conditions or even effects; rather, it is a heterogeneous, hybrid, uneven and shifting beast. What I wanted to contest in their arguments is the notion that neoliberalism,

Chapter 4. Assetization and the Concentration of Economic Power

even as a process, is something we can actually identify; if it is hybrid, if it is uneven, if it is uneven, how do we actually know it is neoliberalization and not another process? At some point we have to make an assumption and then support our claim with our arguments. In relation to neoliberalism, however, I think the concept of 'neoliberalization' misses some of the specific changes that have occurred since the mid-twentieth century.

What we have to appreciate is that *the economy* is not a 'real' thing waiting out there for us to discover and explain by observing what happens when people engage in economic activity. The economy is a construction of our daily decisions *and* – this is vital – the ideas we use to explain the reasons, effects and relationships about these decisions. In this sense trying to find the optimal market conditions is really an attempt to assert how markets *should* operate rather than how they *do* operate – it's a confusion of should and is. This is an intellectual trap that economists seem to frequently fall into, largely because of their underpinning theoretical and conceptual assumptions (e.g. rational self-interest, methodological individualism, etc.). The problem with this approach is that it leads to self-fulfilling prophecies;[48] e.g. an economist comes up with a theory about the economy that they think reflects optimal market conditions or decisions, and then they try to implement it *even if*, to their surprise, they find that the world is not like their theory or model. This is what happened with agency theory when it came to corporate governance. Economists like Jensen and Meckling, Fama and so on thought that existing forms of corporate governance were inefficient and needed to be changed to fit their theoretical perspective. As they convinced corporate managers, investors, analysts etc. their theory became embedded in the decision-making of these social actors; it became real as a result of these decisions. Now, economic decisions do not need to reflect accurately or completely the theories they build on to lead to change, as Dobbin and Jung's work illustrates. Things still change, just not as economists might expect or predict. Hence why they were unable to predict the GFC – it was simply not in their models and theories, nor was it even on their radars as it was so alien to them.[49]

To finish up ... what I wanted to get across in this chapter is that thinking about neoliberalism as a process misses two major things: first, it leaves us with little concrete sense of who is responsible for implementing neoliberal ideas and policies, it could literally be different in every instance; which means that, second, it ignores a key agent of political-economic change over the last half century, the corporation. According to critics of neoliberalism like Peck, Tickell, etc., it is the state that creates markets. What this ignores is that corporations have effectively become like the state, as David Ciepley points out,[50] especially as they became internationalized after WW2. These multinational corporations (MNCs) became massive monopolies, controlling the allocation and distribution of resources within and between countries around the world, as well as the lives and livelihoods of millions of workers, customers, etc. Yet they don't sit *within* traditional political jurisdictions, and hence why various activists, politicians and others raise concerns about oversight, monitoring and so forth; instead they sit *between* and *across* jurisdictions. They operate in different jurisdictions and have to mesh their activities as a functional whole by working out ways to integrate the differences or to supersede them. A company like British Petroleum, for example, has to operate in relation to (a) the British state when it comes to shareholder activities (e.g. stock markets, investor relations, etc.); (b) other national states when it comes to oil exploration, extraction and distribution; and (c) other corporations when they seek to borrow money on the Euromarkets (see Chapter 3). This is a complex web of relations, to say the least. It is also the centre of most economic activity in the Atlantic Heartland as these massive corporations dominate employment, revenues, assets, profits and various other indicators we use to represent healthy economies. Thus, and another point made by Ciepley, corporate monopoly and restructuring has led us to become *more* governed rather than less governed, although in this case it's supposedly private organizations rather than the state doing the governing.

1   This is a point made by Joel Bakan amongst others; see, Bakan, J. (2004) The Corporation. London: Constable. It's also worth reading the work of people like Joshua Barkan who makes a number of interesting arguments about corporate personhood and political sovereignty; see, Barkan, J. (2010) Liberal Government and the Corporate Person. *Journal of Cultural Economy* 3(1): 53-68; and, Barkan, J. (2012) Roberto Esposito's Political Biology and Corporate Forms of Life. *Law, Culture, and the Humanities* 8(1): 84-101.
2   See, for example, Peck, J. and Tickell, A. (2002) Neoliberalizing space. *Antipode* 34(3): 380-404; Tickell, A. and Peck, J. (2003) Making global rules: globalisation or neoliberalization, in J. Peck and H. Yeung (eds) *Remaking the global economy*. London: Sage, pp.163-182; also see others, Brenner, N. and Theodore, N. (2002) Cities and the geographies of 'actually existing neoliberalism'. *Antipode* 34(3): 356-386; Springer, S. (2010) Neoliberalism and Geography: Expansions, Variegations, Formations. *Geography Compass* 4 (8): 1025-1038; and, Springer, S. (2012) Neoliberalism as discourse: between Foucauldian political economy and Marxian poststructuralism. *Critical Discourse Studies* 9(2): 133-147.
3   Tickell and Peck, 'Making global rules', note 2, p.166.
4   Peck and Tickell, 'Neoliberalizing space', note 2, p.383.
5   Birch, K. and Mykhnenko, V. (2009) Varieties of neoliberalism? Restructuring in large industrially-dependent regions across Western and Eastern Europe. *Journal of Economic Geography* 9(3): 355-380; Cerny, P. (2008)

Embedding neoliberalism: the evolution of a hegemonic paradigm. *The Journal of International Trade and Diplomacy* 2: 1–46; Fourcade-Gourinchas, M. and Babb, S. (2002) The Rebirth of the Liberal Creed: Paths to Neoliberalism in Four Countries. *American Journal of Sociology* 108 (3):533-579; Jessop, B. (2010) From hegemony to crisis?: The continuing ecological dominance of neo-liberalism, in Birch, K. & Mykhnenko, V. (eds.) *The Rise and Fall of Neoliberalism: The Collapse of an Economic Order?* London: Zed Books, p. 177-187; Larner, W. (2003) Neoliberalism? *Environment and Planning D: Society and Space* 21(5): 309-312; and, Prasad, M. (2006) *The Politics of Free Markets*. Chicago: University of Chicago Press.

6 Hodgson, G. (2005) Knowledge at work: Some neoliberal anachronisms. Review of Social Economy 63(4): 547-565.

7 Definition taken from, http://www.iasplus.com/en/standards/standard37

8 Veblen, T. (1908) On the nature of capital: Investment, intangible assets, and the pecuniary magnate. *Journal of Economics* 23(1): p.121.

9 Crouch, C. (2011) *The Strange Non-Death of Neoliberalism*. Cambridge: Polity, p.115.

10 There is a huge literature out there on the incorporation of intellectual property rights (IPRs) in the World Trade Organization (WTO), or what became known as TRIPS (Trade-related aspects of intellectual property rights). Just a couple of examples include: Drahos, P. and Braithwaite, J. (2002) *Informational Feudalism*. London: Earthscan; and, David Tyfield who outlines how US multinationals, especially from the pharmaceutical sector, actively lobbied the US government to include IP protection under WTO rules; see Tyfield, D. (2008) Enabling TRIPs: The pharma-biotech-university patent coalition. *Review of International Political Economy* 15(4): 535-566.

Chapter 4. Assetization and the Concentration of Economic Power

11 See, for example, Zhang, Y., Andrew, J. and Rudkin, K. (2012) Accounting as an instrument of neoliberalisation? Exploring the adoption of fair value accounting in China. *Accounting, Auditing and Accountability Journal* 25(8): 1-29.
12 MacKenzie, D. (2009) *Material Markets*. Oxford: Oxford University Press.
13 Deutschman, C. (2011) Limits to financialization: Sociological analyses of the financial crisis. *European Journal of Sociology* 52(3): p.354.
14 See, Krippner, G. (2005) The financialization of the American economy. *Socio-Economic Review* 3: 173-208; and, Palley, T. (2007) *Financialization: What It Is and Why It Matters*. Levy Economics Institute: Economics Working Paper Archive Working Paper 525.
15 Data available online: http://www.bis.org/statistics/credtopriv.htm and http://stats.oecd.org/Index.aspx?QueryId=350#
16 Brenner, R. (2009) *What is Good for Goldman Sachs is Good for America: The Origins of the Current Crisis*, available online: http://www.sscnet.ucla.edu/issr/cstch/papers/BrennerCrisisTodayOctober2009.pdf
17 Data available online: http://www.nationwide.co.uk/hpi/datadownload/data_download.htm
18 Watson, M. (2010) House Price Keynesianism and the Contradictions of the Modern Investor Subject. *Housing Studies* 25(3): p.421.
19 Lazzarato, M. (2012) *The Making of the Indebted Man*. San Francisco: Semiotext(e).
20 Duménil, G. and Lévy, D. (2011) *The Crisis of Neoliberalism*. Cambridge, MA: Harvard University Press, Ch.7-8.
21 Palma, J. (2009) The revenge of the market on the rentiers: Why neo-liberal reports of the end of history turned out to be premature. *Cambridge Journal of Economics* 33: p.834.
22 Blyth, M. (2013) *Austerity*. Oxford: Oxford University Press.

23 Walks, A. (2010) Bailing Out the Wealthy: Responses to the Financial Crisis, Ponzi Neoliberalism, and the City. *Human Geography*. 3 (3): 54-84.

24 Indiviglio, D. (2011) Chart of the Day: Student Loans Have Grown 511% Since 1999. *The Atlantic* (18 August 2011), available online: http://www.theatlantic.com/business/archive/2011/08/chart-of-the-day-student-loans-have-grown-511-since-1999/243821/

25 For a discussion of Occupy and other 'resistance' movements to austerity see, Worth, O. (2013) *Resistance in the Age of Austerity*. London: Zed Books.

26 Chakrabortty, A. (2013) Raise interest rates on old student loans, secret report proposes. *The Guardian* (13 June), available online: http://www.guardian.co.uk/money/2013/jun/13/raise-interest-rate-student-loans-secret-report

27 Veblen, 'On the nature of capital', note 8, p.116.

28 Examples include, Lazarrato, M. (1997) *Lavoro Immateriale e Soggettivita*. Verona: Ombre corte; and, Morini, C. and Fumagalli, A. (2010) Life put to work: Towards a life theory of value. *ephemera*, 10(3/4): 234-255.

29 Boutang, Y.M. (2011) *Cognitive Capitalism*, Cambridge: Polity, p.14.

30 Marazzi, C. (2011) *The Violence of Financial Capitalism*. Los Angeles: semiotext(e).

31 Taibbi, M. (2011) *Griftopia*. New York: Spiegel and Gau Trade Paperbacks.

32 Lazonick, W. and O'Sullivan, M. (2000) Maximizing Shareholder Value: A New Ideology for Corporate Governance. *Economy and Society* 29(1): 13-35.

33 Some examples include, Alchian, A. and Demsetz, H. (1972) Production, Information Costs, and Economic Organization. *The American Economic Review* 62(5): 777–795; Jensen, M. and Meckling, W. (1976) Theory of the firm: Managerial behavior, agency costs and ownership structure. *Journal of*

Chapter 4. Assetization and the Concentration of Economic Power

Financial Economies 3: 305-360; and, Fama, E. (1980) Agency Problems and the Theory of the Firm. *Journal of Political Economy* 88(2): 288-307.

34 Khurana, R. (2007) *From Higher Aims to Hired Hands: The Social Transformation of American Business Schools and the Unfulfilled Promise of Management as a Profession.* Princeton: Princeton University Press; and, Locke, R. and Spender, J-C. (2011) *Confronting Managerialism.* London: Zed Books.

35 Dobbin, F, and Jung, J. (2010) The Misapplication of Mr. Michael Jensen: How Agency Theory Brought Down the Economy and Why it Might Again, in M. Lounsbury and P. Hirsch (eds) *Markets on Trial: The Economic Sociology of the U.S. Financial Crisis.* Bingley: Emerald, pp.29-64.

36 Definition taken from: http://www.iasplus.com/en/standards/ias38

37 OECD (2012) *New Sources of Growth: Knowledge-based Capital Driving Investment and Productivity in the 21st Century.* Paris: Organisation for Economic Cooperation and Development.

38 Palma, 'The revenge of the market on the rentiers', note 21.

39 Available online: http://www.oceantomo.com/productsand-services/investments/intangible-market-value

40 Leadbeater, C. (1999) *Living on Thin Air: The New Economy.* London: Penguin, p.viii.

41 See this survey of the economic literature, Shleifer, A. and Vishny, R. (1997) A survey of corporate governance. *The Journal of Finance* 52(2): 737-783.

42 Davis, G. (2008) A new finance capitalism? Mutual funds and ownership re-concentration in the United States. *European Management Review* 5(1): 11-21.

43 For a discussion of a range of forms of corporate governance, see Letza, S., Sun, X. and Kirkbride, J. (2004) Shareholding versus stakeholding: a critical review of corporate governance. *Corporate Governance: An International Review* 12(3): 242-262.

44 Crouch, *The Strange Non-death of Neoliberalism*, note 9, p.100.
45 According to Ronen Palan, 'goodwill' is of particular importance because it represents the capitalization of businesses as 'going concerns' – that is, as businesses expected to make future earnings. Without this expectation a business would lose significant value because the value of its assets would only represent their value at liquidation (e.g. when sold for scrap) rather than as productive assets: see, Palan, R. (2012) The financial crisis and intangible value: Preliminary remarks. Paper presented at the *SPERI Inaugural Conference*, University of Sheffield.
46 Blyth, *Austerity*, note 22.
47 Dobbin and Jung, 'The Misapplication of Mr. Michael Jensen', note 35.
48 Ferraro, F., Pfeffer, J. and Sutton, R. (2005) Economics Language and Assumptions: How Theories Can Become Self-fulfilling. *Academy Of Management Review* 30: 8-24.
49 See, Mirowski, P. (2010) The Great Mortification: Economists' Responses to the Crisis of 2007-(and counting). *The Hedgehog Review* 12(2): 28-41.
50 The work of David Ciepley is interesting here as he discusses the political position of corporations in modern society – basically he points out that corporations are like 'private' states since they govern workers, engage in diplomacy with suppliers, etc.: see, Ciepley, D. (2013) Beyond Public and Private: Toward a Political Theory of the Corporation. *American Political Science Review* 107(1): 139-158.

Chapter 5

Manifesto for a Doomed Youth

Introduction

In this chapter I focus on the target of recent popular criticism, namely the top 1% of income earners and wealth holders. It would be hard to have missed the condemnation of the richest members of society since the global financial crisis (GFC), even if our rulers have signally failed to do anything about it. Examples of protest range across the political divide from the American Tea Party to the worldwide Occupy movement – Owen Worth even argues that political protest has been more evident on the right rather than the left.[1] However, it is necessary, in order to identify a target, to outline what it is about the top 1% that makes them so revolting – pun intended!

I'll therefore start by rehashing the existing arguments about the negative effects of rising inequality and domination by the top 1% over our societies, economies and lives. I need to show you how the top 1% have supposedly managed to remake society in their own interests, and their own image. This involves a cold, hard look at our own choices and decisions, which is essential if we want to understand our own complicity in the rise of the top 1% – and I don't think "complicity" is too strong a word. We have to understand how so many people have been enrolled in this destructive transformation. Basically, I'm going to make the point that the top 1% have not got where they are without our help; sometimes this has been conscious and sometimes it have been unintentional, but in each case it can be challenged and resisted if we so choose. And to be clear, I'm not giving leftist activists, teachers and scholars a free pass on this front, we have all been complicit.

From this analysis I end the chapter with a manifesto for

change. Its aims are, perhaps, modest in that I want to start with very small acts to engender social change, but it's also meant to encourage new perspectives rather than be overly prescriptive. In foregrounding this manifesto, I want you, as the reader, to go away with a more optimistic sense of what we can do to change the world, rather than simply be overwhelmed by the image of 'neoliberalism' – or whatever it is – as a bloated, decaying zombie crouching above all our bodies, feeding on the corpse of our economies and societies even as it slowly rots. One starting point, building on the previous chapters, is to think about how dependent the main governing institutions of our time – the corporation – is on our experiences, skills, education, beliefs, tastes, friendships, cultural values, and so on. At every point in our lives we can find holes, gaps, weak spots, spaces where we might wage a guerrilla defence against the 'free' market and, more crucially, against monopoly, or even where we might mount outright assaults on the bastions of corporate power.

Inequality, Plutocracy and the Top 1%

In the Atlantic Heartland it is obvious that inequality has worsened over the last few decades. If nothing else there is ample evidence of rising and incessant 'aspirational' visions staring back at us from billboards, television advertising and social media. What is perhaps less clear, at least in the mainstream and until activists and others have started banging on about it, is the re-emergence of a capitalist elite hell-bent on extracting every last ounce of profit from their investments in various assets – the fictional figure of Gordon Gecko and his motto of "greed is good" from the 1987 film *Wall Street* loom over the changes that have happened to our economies. While we might wish to identify this as 'neoliberal', such terms are almost moot considering our collective ability to condemn, in the strongest terms, life in a world where some individuals can spend over $300,000 on a *round* of champagne,[2] while a quarter of the American population struggles on less than 10% of that amount each year. What is worrying, in my view, is the distortions this causes in our perceptions of reality, which is ably illustrated on YouTube,[3] and the policies pursued by our governments who are in hock to an elite few.[4]

Inequality Like Never Before?
What we have here is an inequality that boggles the mind when we put it in these terms. We are now back to inequalities last seen during the Gilded Age in the 1920s as evident in Figure 3.1 in Chapter 3. All of this is down to some very simple dynamics underpinning the assetization of our economies. Wage-inflation has given way to asset-inflation, which means falling wages for the majority but rising wages and asset values for the minority. This is evident in stagnating average real wages across the Anglo-American economies since the 1970s. A 2011 report published by the *Resolution Foundation* highlights the fact that the share of national income received by workers in the UK, USA and Canada has fallen by 5.3%, 3.1% and 3.8% respectively between 1970 and 2007.[5] America represents the clearest example of this unequal sharing of national wealth. According to Jose Palma, for example, the average income growth of the top 1% in the USA was 10.3% between 1993-2000 and 11% between 2002-2006 compared with 2.2% and 0.3% for the *bottom 90%*. The income of the top 1% grew at an almost fivefold-rate during 1993-2000 and at a 30-fold rate in 2002-2006 compared with 90% of Americans.[6] Such numbers are astonishing; how did we get to this state? It's no wonder that people are so angry, although why they weren't angry before the global financial crisis (GFC) is worth thinking about.

In order to legitimate this sort of huge inequality, there are two forms of 'free' market or, more accurately, *free-the-monopolies* narrative at work. On the one hand, and as covered in Chapter 2, there is a concern with monetary stability, exemplified by the shifting focus from unemployment to inflation as the key societal danger. This not only legitimates rising interest rates, nominal and, more importantly, real, it also legitimates the *effects* of these rising interest rates – including rising unemployment, falling wages, trade union repression, wage moderation, etc. It also justifies, into the bargain, the opening up of the national economies of the USA, UK and Canada to international competitive pressures from countries where labour costs are so much cheaper. As mentioned already, this leads to the stagnation of average wages, particularly *real* average wages. For example, David Harvey argues that average real wages in the USA stood at $15.72 per hour in 1973 but then fell to $14.15 by 2000.[7] Harvey identified a similar trend in the UK in a later book.[8] What is most egregious, however, is that accompanying these stagnant average wages are sky-rocketing wages for the top 1% since 1978, outlined by Jose Palma and something I'll come back to below when I discuss the impacts of these changes.

On the other hand, the *free-the-monopolies* narrative has naturalized individual and personal forms of responsibility over collective action. As a result, responsibility has been downloaded onto individuals who are incentivized to buy into the idea of housing and pensions as forms of welfare insurance,[9] while simultaneously borrowing to the hilt in order to do so (see Figure 4.2 in last chapter). This was meant to signal the emergence of an 'ownership society' – a perspective extolled by the likes of Margaret Thatcher back in the 1980s and still going strong today.[10] As Thatcher and others realized, an ownership society was built on household and consumer debt and borrowing, which has taken off as a percentage of GDP since the 1980s in the USA, UK and Canada. There are other ways to characterize this shift, however. Some like Matthew Watson describe it as "house-price Keynesianism" – consumption funded by house price increases – while others like Colin Crouch see it in broader terms as "privatized Keynesianism" – household borrowing, by you and I, to fund our spending and aggregate demand.[11] This is not necessarily neoliberal, in either ideology or policy terms. What it does mean, however, is that while everybody has become tied into the assetization of our societies and economies, some have benefited more than others, but most people who could partake (and not everyone could obviously) found some way to benefit from rising asset prices.

This is the major downside with assetization. It is, in the words of Alan Walks,[12] as if we have blindly walked into a massive "giant Ponzi system" – we borrow to buy houses and other assets, which will only gain in value if we can convince those people behind us to want to buy the same things and then encourage them to borrow to do so. With this in mind, it is hardly surprising that a growing number of people in the Atlantic Heartland actually supported – and still support – politicians who publicly argued for the need to rein in rising wage-inflation, which was caused – at least in common parlance – by Keynesian policies and trade union wage demands. This wage-inflation directly threatened a growing number of people's assets and the asset-inflation they needed to ensure they captured the benefits of their assets, whether this was their pensions or their houses. I'll come back to this issue when I discuss how the top 1% got away with it all; basically, they had help from the rest of us, or at least those people with ample assets to protect.

Plutocracy – Rule by the Rich
Recently the Harvard economist Greg Mankiw, somewhat of a *bête noire* to leftist activist groups like *Adbuster* magazine, wrote a piece lauding the contribution of the top 1% to our economies.[13] Mankiw argues that inequality and especially the rising incomes of the top 1% are better explained by the "earnings gap between skilled and unskilled workers" (p.4). Now, Mankiw equates people like Steve Jobs or Bill Gates with

everyday software engineers, assuming that the top 1% are merely "skilled workers" rather than major asset holders. What Mankiw's argument illustrates, if nothing else, is how to go about legitimating inequality as "efficient" or beneficial – just like corporate monopoly (see Chapter 3). This makes the crumbs thrown to the rest of us on the back of rising and highly skewed income growth look like the gifts of benevolent overlords, while ignoring the dependence of most people on easy credit and consequent debts of various kinds (e.g. mortgage, student loan, credit card, etc.). Such debt, in turn, comes to form the assets of the top 1% who find it more profitable to use their money to buy assets rather than productive (and job-creating) investments. Gradually we'll find that all parts of our lives have been capitalized as assets that can be purchased by the top 1% to earn them an income that can be securitized, then bet on as a speculative derivative (see Chapter 4). With hindsight, what is most galling about this is that when it all comes crashing down, as it did in 2007-08, then governments around the world step in to prop up the incomes and wealth of this top 1% by using everyone else's tax payments – as John Lanchester suggests, we can't even recover jobs and wages until we pay off the banks.[14]

We have to ask, what would make governments take notice of a majority rather than the top 1%? Without debt, our economies would largely cease to function since it would lead to severe limits on house purchasing and consumption – the two driving forces of the UK, USA and Canadian economies. We have to think beyond the financial sector if we want to challenge this myopia, especially as more and more of our lives are capitalized as assets. Part of the problem is that both the rising incomes of the top 1% and wider economic growth have now been decoupled from income growth amongst the majority of the population. Demand is no longer being driven by wage rises, nor is investment capital coming from the savings of the majority – so what would make governments take notice of us in light of this shift? It's a hard question to stomach, considering the implications. However, it is not as simply as all this. If we go back to the discussion in the last chapter about institutional investors it is obvious that most people's mutual, insurance and pensions funds are tied into the continuation of this economic system. Our lives are intimately tied to the expansion of the income and wealth of the top 1% through the systemic entanglement of our financial assets with their financial assets. While we cannot leverage ours, they can use ours to leverage – or at least they could until the GFC – theirs and ours to reap huge returns while spreading risk to us and insuring themselves against risks to themselves.

Perhaps the most egregious impact of assetization then is the erosion of collective action as a viable political-economic response to societal problems and challenges, except those that threaten the wealth of the top 1% of course. We can ask whether this erosion caused the assetization of our economies or if the reverse is true, but this probably misses the point. It is likely that the erosion of collective action and the shift to an asset-based economy happened at the same time and reinforced each other. This dual process has entailed falling wage-income at the same time as it has involved a significant expansion of pension, mutual and insurance funds, which are managed by institutional investors – see the work of Erturk and colleagues for more details on this.[15] The latter represents a shift from collective forms of protection exemplified by the welfare state – which is supported through wage-income whether from general taxation or social insurance – towards financialized forms of personal insurance increasingly subsidized by government and business as part of employment packages and social policies.

This brings me to the frequently confusing part of the story; what is the state still doing in the picture? Popular commentators and journalists frequently equate neoliberalism with the rolling back or hollowing out of the state, exemplified by the call for limits to government intervention in the economy. But this misses the point entirely. The state is deeply implicated in all that has happened; it has heavily subsidized the assetization of our economies. As I showed in Chapter 2 the supposedly neoliberal governments of the 1980s – and then 1990s and 2000s – in the UK, USA and Canada all ended up increasing public spending at one point or another. According to the work of Peter Jackson,[16] for example, the proportion of government outlays to GDP rose across all three countries between 1970 and 1995 before falling back by 2004 – see Figure 5.1.

FIGURE 5.1: Government Outlays in the USA, UK and Canada (% GDP)

COUNTRY	1970	1980	1990	2004
Canada	33.8	39.1	46	37.2
United Kingdom	36.7	43	41.9	39.7
United States of America	29.6	31.3	33.6	31.3

Source: Peter Jackson (2009) The Size and Scope of the Public Sector: An International Comparison, in T. Bovaird and E. Loffler (eds) *Public Sector Management Handbook* (2nd Edition). London: Routledge.

Considering that this government spending was undertaken as top tax rates were lowered, unemployment and foreign competition reduced wages, and welfare systems were restructured, it is evident why public debt kept rising (see Chapter 2) and why government spending (borrowed from top earners) became a way to subsidize assetization – see Box 5.1 for details of other ways governments in the Atlantic Heartland have subsidized asset-based economies. Asking what might make governments rethink their policies is critical, in my opinion. There are no reasons why governments won't simply rationalize their actions in light of the dominance of the top 1% in our various economies,

Chapter 5. Manifesto for a Doomed Youth

as with elsewhere around the world. Thus we have to deal with the fact we currently live in a *plutocracy* and not a democracy. It's the ideas, interests and demands of the top 1% that currently dominate politicians' and policy-makers' minds; it's not the needs of the majority, or of proponents of alternatives to capitalism, or even of conservatives demanding an end to government intervention and central banking.

Box 5.1 Assetization and the State

- Governments borrowed more so they could lower tax rates, thereby creating public debt which becomes an asset to its holder.
- Governments borrowed from the wealthiest, rather than taxing them, driving up asset values.
- Governments sold off state assets as part of programs promoting the privatization and marketization of public industries, utilities, social housing, and infrastructure, often at under-valued or heavily discounted prices and to the wealthiest members of society.
- Governments expanded subsidies to home owners (e.g. mortgage tax relief, mortgage insurance, interest tax deductions, etc.).
- Governments subsidized banks and the financial sector through collective insurance for private risk-taking, exemplified by the GFC.
- Governments have eroded the welfare state, forcing people to turn to individual forms of social insurance and asset-based forms of welfare (e.g. housing, savings).

Sources: Watson, M. (2008) Constituting Monetary Conservatives via the 'Savings Habit': New Labour and the

> British Housing Market Bubble. *Comparative European Politics* 6(3): 285-304; Lanchester, J. (2010) *IOU*. Toronto: McClelland and Stewart; Whitfield, D. (2010) *Global Auction of Public Assets*. Nottingham: Spokesman; MacKenzie, D. (2013) The Magic Lever. *London Review of Books* 35(9): 16-19.

How the Top 1% Got Away with It

How did it end this way? As we return to another Gilded Age at the end of the twentieth and start of the twenty-first centuries,[17] why has this not caused mass and popular outrage all along? Once it all became obvious that the actions of the banks and top 1% had screwed the rest of us, we saw evidence of rising anger in the form of movements like the Tea Party in America and the Occupy Movement around the world, but before that we didn't hear so much as a squeak in mainstream political or popular debates. It's not as if rising inequality was happening elsewhere, somewhere overseas we could ignore all too easily. It was all around us, if we chose to look. Inequality is most evident in countries like the USA, UK and Canada. In fact, the U-shape trend in inequality across the Atlantic Heartland is unique, in many ways, when compared with other countries in the Global North. Countries in Scandinavia and continental Europe have not witnessed the same levels of income inequality in the same period of time, which raises several questions. Why the difference? What can we do about it? Is neoliberalism responsible? Is it all the fault of the top 1%? My answer to the last of these is that it's not, we all bear some responsibility in one way or another – well, in one way specifically.

Housing and Rising Inequality
As many people may have noticed, TV shows about housing – selling them, doing them up, flipping them, etc. – have quietly

slunk from our screens since 2007. What many now call "housing porn" is merely the cultural expression of what makes all of us responsible in some ways for what happened and how the top 1% got away with it. They did it with our help, basically. As people in the US, UK and Canada increasingly bought into the home-owner dream – now nightmare for many – from the 1970s onwards, they also increasingly bought into a set of ideas about how our economies should be run; that is, keep wage-inflation low, bump up asset-inflation and home-owners win every time – well, until recently. The increasing obsession we have with home-ownership – which is itself a heavily loaded term but easier to write than "housing ownership" – is directly implicated in rising inequality levels. As usual I can't claim to be the first to identify this. Others, including journalists at *The Huffington Post* website,[18] make similar arguments. Nor am I making this claim only in relation to the sub-prime mortgage lending that so many people blame for the GFC. What I'm claiming is that inequality is directly tied into rising home-ownership rates across the US, UK and Canada, which have risen to about 70% of households since the 1970s.

As should be obvious from my arguments so far, I see this expansion of home-ownership as part of a broader emergence of asset-based economies in the Atlantic Heartland. Now this has not been a smooth ride. As Mark Blyth points out, the financial sector has been riding a series of "global asset bubbles using huge amounts of leverage" since the 1980s. First, there was a bubble in share prices starting in 1987, which was followed by a bubble in real estate from 1997 and then a commodities bubble from 2005 onwards. While the equity and housing bubbles ended in 2007, the commodities bubble has continued since the start of the GFC.[19] What Blyth illustrates is the dependence of our economies on the expansion of assets held by or held on behalf of the general populace, for want of a better word. Home-ownership rates have increased, expanding the housing market, as has the ownership of equity and other financial assets by institutional investors like pension, mutual and insurance funds (see last chapter). As asset-holders, we – and I mean "we" in the broadest sense – have turned against wage-inflation because it threatens to erode our asset wealth. This is what William Greider argued in *Secrets of the Temple* back in 1987; the monetarist turn in the 1970s can be seen as a revolt by asset-holders and savers against real and imagined wage-inflation.[20] Consequently there has been a *popular* turn against the quasi-Keynesian policies pursued since WW2 and not just an elite revolt.

Inflation caused by Keynesian policies threatened people's investments in assets like housing, pensions, mutual funds, and so on – more details are contained in Chapter 2. Inflation eroded the value of these assets, especially during the 1970s when real interest rates plummeted below 0% across the US, UK and Canada – see Figure 2.8. The effects of this were slightly contradictory. On the one hand, it enabled more people to borrow money because the value of debt was eroded significantly by inflation, but only until interest rates were raised to curb inflation in the early 1980s. After interest rates rose, the value of debt increased in real terms providing a nice new source of income for banks, etc. – see Figure 2.7. On the other hand, it threatened to erode the value of anything bought by people. So, it was necessary to carefully balance borrowing with the buying of assets, but since the latter had started well before the 1970s, inflation became more of a threat than boon. What this meant was that 'neoliberal' ideas, especially those of monetarists like Milton Friedman, became very attractive, at least politically if not practically. The idea of price stability appeared to make sense in light of shifting ownership (up and 'good') and wage (up and 'bad') trends. Thus it's understandable that wage-inflation – what we think of as general inflation nowadays – was so demonized, while asset-inflation – what we now think of as beneficial – was and is lauded as a growth stimulant (but only because it is allied to consumer debt).

Buying into the Housing Delusion
As I've grown older, I've encountered a dominant and taken-for-granted assumption that I will buy a house and get on the fantastical property ladder – it's not even framed as "I should" buy a house, it is simply understood that as I grow older "I will want" to buy a house. Sometimes people find it quite threatening when I tell them I don't want to buy a house, especially when I outline why this is so. This view is even prevalent amongst leftist scholars and activists, many of whom fail to challenge prevailing societal delusions with their own actions. To me it's more than strange that we all buy into the mass hysteria of home-ownership; it's also socially unjust. While the bottom half of society benefited most from rising wages in the post-WW2 era, the top half (or more) have done usurped this position since the 1970s when their assets (e.g. housing) appreciated in value at the expense of wages – of course, the (upper-) middle classes and top 1% have benefited most. The key consequence of this reversal is that the link between living standards and wages has, for most people at least, been severed. This flip from rising wages to rising assets in the 1970s is not inevitable, nor does it reflect some arcane workings of *the* economy; it involves decisions made by politicians, by voters, by savers, by house buyers, by all of us in one way or another.

In order to maintain rising living standards, most people since the 1970s have turned to debt in all its wonderful forms – see David Graeber for a history of debt.[21] Some people have benefited from their borrowing (e.g. house owners), while others have turned to it out of necessity (e.g. credit cards) or in the hope of improving their lives (e.g. students). It is the former, however, who have benefited from the wealth effect as their borrowing capacity has been extended by the rising value of their assets (i.e. collateral). What this has led to is American, British and

Canadian governments – of all political hues and stripes – promoting home-ownership and the housing market as a means to economic growth by default; that is, as the result of rising asset values rather than wage increases enabling more household borrowing. As I mentioned above, this has been variously described as "house-price Keynesianism" and "privatized Keynesianism", but it isn't necessarily a form of neoliberalism. It's stimulus in another form. Now, the problem with this deliberate policy of stoking housing markets is that it depends on continuously rising asset values and people buying into the idea that home-ownership is the be-all-and-end-all of life. Rising real wages are no longer important if you can get on the housing ladder and, crucially, climb ever upwards towards ... well, that's never really clear.

It seems entirely rational for people to buy into this vision, especially since the early 1980s when stagnant wages kicked in and assets kicked ever upwards. House prices have risen significantly since the 1980s, despite a brief dip in the early 1990s, until 2007 – see Figure 4.3 for example. However, this housing delusion is not as simply as it may first appear:

> **First:** A mortgage does not mean you *own* a house nor does it mean *you* have an asset. The mortgage lender owns your house and you have a liability to pay back the mortgage; hence, it is their asset since it provides them with an income from your interest (and principal) repayments. It only becomes your asset once it is repaid in full, although you may build up significant *equity* in it before then (you may also end up in negative equity though). However, by the time you are paying down a mortgage (in your 30s and 40s) you will probably need to access that illiquid equity to pay for your children's higher education, or maybe your own medical bills if you live in the USA, or maybe just those holidays you think you deserve. Effectively then what you are doing is putting

Chapter 5. Manifesto for a Doomed Youth

away money so you can borrow it in another form against your house as collateral, creating yet another asset for the financial warlocks to play with. This is going to get worse in the future as governments provide fewer collective goods – some of which is the result of current austerity policies pursued to resolve the problems caused by banks. Oh happy days!

Second: The gains in the house prices you expect from buying a house are not as significant as you may first think. In dissecting this apparent wealth revolution many people have bought into, John Lanchester argues in his book *I.O.U.* that rising house prices have actually done little better than other long-term investments once inflation is taken into account. However, houses remain the key 'asset' most people have or can acquire, at least outside of the top 1%, because lenders are subsidized and insured against bad housing debts.

What our housing obsession has seemingly done, though, is change what we value as citizens. It has led to the rise of investor citizens, or crown subjects if you live in the UK and Canada, and the spread of *fiscal conservatism* as a default attitude – that is, we must be concerned with low inflation and wage moderation or we'll end up with rising interest rates we cannot afford (and that limit our ability to cash out) and houses which lose their real value as prices are eroded by inflation. We've basically ended up in a political-economic system that militates against rising real wages and rising livings standards for the poorer members of society because to do so would threaten the value of the assets (e.g. houses, pensions, etc.) of the wealthier members of society. And here I'm not talking about the top 1%, I mean the nearly 70% of households that are owner-occupiers. Underlying owner-occupation are the income streams that feed the top 1%; all the interest payments on mortgages, credit cards, personal debt, etc.

provide the top 1% with its succour as they manage *our* institutional investment funds in our names, if not to our benefit. Ultimately, we are left with the majority of people concerned more with making sure that no one threatens rising asset values and makes sure that the value of those assets rises faster than wage-inflation – that is, our salaries and wages.

What I think is important to highlight is that most people are complicit with the rule of the top 1%, whether this is intentional or not is beside the point. The transformation of our economies since the 1970s has been built on a delusional narrative of housing ownership, alongside other assets. This delusion necessitates stagnant real wages in order to ensure that house price inflation rises faster than general inflation, all of which creates a warm fuzzy feeling amongst home-owners – "my house is more valuable than last year so I am better off". While many home-owners have seemingly done very well out of this, and how could they not considering all the subsidies that have been thrown at them, the top 1% have done even better. In contrast, many other people have suffered – this includes those excluded from borrowing altogether; those with low wages; those forced to live on welfare; and those with no inter-generational assets to climb on-board the property party bus. It is hardly surprising that inequality is rising across the US, UK and Canada considering that these property disparities enable some parents to pass on their privilege to their children through the ability to borrow to pay for things private schools, university tuition, first-home down payments, and so on.

A Manifesto for a Doomed Youth

This brings me to the main purpose of this chapter. Above I've outlined the effects of everything I've written about elsewhere in this book and how the top 1% managed to get away with so much. What we are left with is the possibility that future generations of American, Brits and Canadians will be paying off the public, private and corporate debts built up over the last few years as a consequence of the bailouts of all the financial institutions and their employees, executives and shareholders. It is not going to be the privileged baby boomers or even Generation X-ers – myself included, if I'm honest – who feel the pain, despite being the ones who benefited most from the transformation of our societies into asset-based economies. We've got our houses, our pensions, our well-paid jobs. It will be you, the so-called "millennials" born in the last two to three decades who will bear the brunt of the adjustment – on top of which you will face possible environmental catastrophe and fossil fuel bubble unless our governments get off their collective arses and do something about it, and soon.[22] It seems hardly fair. Don't buy into this crap, you don't have to.

While a lot of what has happened is not the fault or responsibility of boomers and X-ers, we are complicit in the direction our societies have headed. As the rest of this book attests, there are deeply systemic and inter-dependent causes of the GFC which people were neither aware of nor thought possible or just did not figure in their models and equations (see Chapter 4). What we have witnessed is the expansion of corporate power driven by a *free-the-monopolies* mentality totally at odds with the early neoliberal thinkers and their conception of free markets. This isn't any person's fault, nor can it be. That being said, a growing proportion of the population in the USA, UK and Canada have bought into the delusions of economists, politicians, think-tankers, commentators, academics and others who should really know better. And this has a direct impact on you, the doomed youth of the sub-title of this book. On the one hand you can become willing dupes in the Ponzi scheme that is the housing market, and on the other you can become indentured serfs through student loans. All the while, you can strive to find fulfilling and worthwhile employment on a jobs ladder that is being hastily pulled up behind your elders. Maybe there are other options to think about – this is where this chapter comes in.

My suggestion is really rather simple. Refuse to pay interest, refuse to borrow money to finance your lives, stop the cycle of credit. That's my suggestion for future generations; opt out of debt-bondage and servitude. That's it – not very earth shattering, is it? What it does involve is working out how to live your lives in ways that don't prop up the current financial system. This can be done by refusing to support the consumerist paradise (nightmare?) with your 'consumer' labour power, by refusing to borrow to buy, by refusing to pay interest on the debts that underpin the financial system and rest of the economy, by refusing to take on the task of servicing and serving the financial system. Stop borrowing money, stop getting into debt, stop paying interest on those loans, and then see what happens.

Let me start with student loans ...
Last year – 2102 – I paid off the last of my student loan debt incurred between 1995 and 1999 when I was studying at the University of Edinburgh in Scotland. I can give myself a nice pat on the back; home and dry, no more debt. I am no longer beholden to anyone to pay them interest for the pleasure of borrowing 'their' money – well, the money magicked out of thin air by financial institutions too big to bail and too powerful to control (see Chapter 2). I was one of the last lucky ones to go through the British university system without having to pay student fees for my education. Since then, student fees have risen again and again – universities can now charge up to £9000 per year if they so choose and most have done just that. I don't want to get into the stupidity of this policy, others like Professor Stefan Collini have done so much better than I ever could,[23] but rather I want to highlight how these debts have become a mechanism to discipline your aspirations.

The year before I paid off my loans I moved to Canada to teach at York University in Toronto. Before moving to this side of

Chapter 5. Manifesto for a Doomed Youth

the Atlantic (Heartland), I hadn't really appreciated how indebted North American students end up in their pursuit of a university education. Obviously I'd heard horror stories, but not about the systematic indebtedness that most students end up getting into. This has become an increasingly important mainstream issue as evident in recent newspaper series in the *New York Times* and Canada's *Globe and Mail*.[24] It is also an issue that is likely to spread to the UK as a direct result of the government there raising student fees. According to a 2011 story in *USA Today*, student loan debt in the USA passed the $1 trillion mark, surpassing credit card debt.[25] Moreover, government legislation, such as the George W. Bush-era *Bankruptcy Abuse Prevention and Consumer Protection Act* (2005), now means students are unable to discharge this debt through bankruptcy proceedings. Similar, although less draconian, laws exist in the UK and Canada. Now, this is important because there is a very real possibility that student loans are going to become the next sub-prime crisis, although students won't be able to walk away from this debt. What is important though is when – not if – governments decide to raise interest rates. This is exactly what the US government almost allowed to happen recently with their student loans.[26] In Britain the government is attempting to flog off student loans to private financial institutions meaning that they need to let these private firms increase interest on the loans in order to make it an attractive purchase.[27] Consequently, you will find that interest payments are going to increase over the next few decades as a result of these sorts of policies.

All of this might not be a major issue if university education was still a ticket to secure and well-paid employment, but it is not. If you graduated 10, 20 or 30 years ago then university probably did benefit you, but if you just graduated or are going to graduate in the future then a university education will just not cut it anymore. Too many people are getting degrees – or, more likely, well-paid and secure employment opportunities for graduates are simply not out there anymore, despite all the rhetoric about knowledge economies and even though you increasingly need a degree to get any sort of job at all. So, if you are part of the "doomed generation" you are in a double bind. Get a degree or you won't get a job *and* pay far more for it than anyone did in the past, even though it is worth less. At the same time you have to listen to those who got their degrees and opportunity bang on about how valuable a university education is and why that means students should pay for it – not that these people would ever suggest they pay more for theirs through higher income tax. There is a terrible logic at work here; education is turned into an individual benefit when it comes to you on the back of claims made about it when it was a collective good for me and my parents. It is now unlikely to pass on those benefits when it is converted into yet another asset (human capital) you can (or is that must?) purchase and claim the income from. Nor are those who benefited most from it, the boomers and X-ers, ever going to be asked – or offer – to pay for their education even though it benefited them more than it will benefit you.

All the interest on these student loans is going to other people; it's not going back to you or to make the world better for you. One day you may be on the receiving end of someone else's interest payments, but maybe not. There could be another crash before then which wipes out your pensions, savings, house value, or whatever. Think about why you want a university education and if you don't know why then don't go to university, at least at that moment. You have time to work out what you'd like to do and you can always go to university part-time while you work. There is no rush; it's not like there's much waiting for you on the other side anyway.

Which brings me to work and employment ...
Student loans have become a mechanism to create indentured servitude or modern-day serfs according to journalists and

writers like Natalia Antonova, Chris Masaino and Jeffrey Williams.[28] This means that university graduates are now being forced to work to pay off their loans immediately, going for any jobs available no matter their conditions, contractual terms, wage levels, and so on. There is little doubt that this impacts on the benighted idea of moderating wages so dear to all those monetarists out there (see Chapter 2). What is also means, however, is that the chance to work in certain sectors of the economy which pay lower wages, like the public or voluntary sectors, or professions which require more training, like law or medicine, are limited to those graduates with the resources – parental or otherwise – to fund these choices. This situation has already evident in what Sarah Kendzior, columnist at *Al-Jazeera*, has called the "prestige economy".[29] Basically what she is arguing is that most decent graduate-level jobs – or what were once thought of as such – now require people to have undertaken internships or other forms of unpaid labour. In fact, she argues that such internships have become "normalized" as a necessary step on the way to (hopefully) paid employment for most careers. One deeply problematic side-effect of this is that it is the wealthiest members of society who can afford to support their children as they undertake this unpaid work, in some cases even paying for the privilege as the auctioning of a UN intern position illustrates.[30]

The real problem is lack of work, however. Across the Global North, youth unemployment (16-24 year olds) is currently running at levels not seen for generations. Some commentators are actually talking about a 'lost generation' resulting from the GFC – those who entered the labour market when the GFC started and have not been able to get a job since, or at least a job they would want.[31] Young workers in places like Greece, Spain and Portugal are suffering the most with youth unemployment rates around 40-60%, several times the official unemployment rate as the gap widens. In places like the US, UK and Canada, the rate may be lower but the same dynamic applies. Young people coming onto the labour market since the GFC are screwed, to be blunt about it. Doubly screwed, in fact, since you'll face pressure to pay back your student loans while working in low-paid and often temporary positions; if you're lucky enough to find work at all, that is. You could be triply screwed if you're expecting to get on the property ladder as well.

The quality and quantity of work in the Atlantic Heartland is far from promising. In Britain, there is talk of new kinds of *zero-hour* work contracts bumping up official employment rates; these are contracts that guarantee no set hours and, therefore, no set pay. As a 2013 report for by the Resolution Foundation highlights, there are now over 200,000 people on these contracts in the UK, almost double the number in 2006. More importantly, nearly 40% of these people are people aged 16-24.[32] This is not all, however. As anonymous blogger Tyler Durden illustrates on the *Zero Hedge* website, the situation in the US is getting worse. The GFC has led to the destruction of mid-paid jobs and their replacement by low-paid work, meaning that about 40% of all jobs in the US are now low-paid compared with 30% in 1980.[33] More and more jobs are now temporary or agency work. Simply put, there are an increasing number of barriers to entry facing young people as they try to find a decent, let alone well-paid, job. It is not enough that you have done a degree anymore; you probably have to intern for free, and support yourself while you do so (or have rich parents), and you are less likely to find secure and permanent employment than your parents or grandparents.

Not everything is doom and gloom, however. In the last chapter I discussed the rise of intangible assets and how some leftist thinkers have characterized this as the rise of 'cognitive capitalism' or 'immaterial labour'.[34] These thinkers are optimistic about our capacity to find those gaps in capitalism that enable people to make – not find – meaningful work. While it may still involve capitalist dynamics, things like YouTube, Twitter, blogging, etc. offer opportunities for developing your interests into a living. A growing number of people on YouTube, for example, have found ways to leverage their intellect, humour, tastes, knowledge, etc. through subscriptions that enable them to monetize their videos through advertising. As mentioned, this does not challenge the dynamics of capitalism but it might enable people to create new forms of work rather than flog themselves for free through internships or similar. Or, indeed, to become indebted as the result of student loans, credit card debt, etc. At least it means you won't be paying anyone any interest any time soon.

And now housing ...

If you can find yourself a job after all that, your mind might turn to buying a house since this is what you should do, right? The problem now is twofold. On one side, exorbitant and rising house prices in key cities like London, Toronto and New York limit your chance to live in those places except in the most isolated suburbs – which raise other problems around the sustainability of car-dependence as we face the need to change our lifestyles in response to climate change. On the other side, no-one wants to sell to you because they are stuck with an asset that has fallen in value since the GFC. You can either get on-board the Ponzi scheme that is housing and pay over the odds, or pay rent to someone else – both ways mean you are basically paying interest to a bank.

When I call housing a Ponzi scheme, I'm not making some sort of analogy – others like Alan Walks have made this claim as well.[35] The housing market is a classic Ponzi (or pyramid) scheme in all but name. You've probably heard the term Ponzi scheme in relation to people like the investor Bernie Madoff who came unstuck after the GFC caught him out. It's named after Charles Ponzi, an early twentieth century, Italian immigrant to the USA, who conned people into investing in a scheme to redeem international postage coupons – I know, go look it up on the internet. By promising more than he could actually deliver to investors, Ponzi managed to attract an enormous amount of investor interest. What Ponzi actually did was pay old investors with money from new investors, without actually generating any income from his scheme, or not enough to deliver the returns he promised. When you think about it, that is exactly what the housing market is like.

Let's imagine buying a house back in the 1970s, or shortly thereafter. Getting on the property ladder back then would mean that you would then be able to sell your house a few years later and move into a bigger property by simply cashing in on the rising value of your house (i.e. your asset's capital gain). At each new stage of the property ladder you accrue further capital gains, enabling you to move upwards once again. In the Atlantic Heartland up until 2007 house prices had been rising continuously since the late 1990s. According to Mark Blyth, for example, there was a housing bubble from 1997 until 2006 in the USA when house prices doubled.[36] A similar trend is evident in Canada as well, according to Alan Walks.[37] If we look further back, as shown in Figure 4.2 in the last chapter, it's possible to see that UK house prices, for example, rose from an average of £22,600 in 1980 to £59,500 in 1990 to £77,600 in 2000 and £184,000 at their peak in the third quarter of 2007. While house prices have been rising since the early 1970s, what really spurred them ever upwards from the early 1980s was falling inflation, a trend which boosted the *real* value of housing as an asset.

Now, it's not just the supposedly monetarist combating of inflation that ensured rising house prices. These prices are dependent on the creation – or social (re-)production – of future home buyers. Home owners need first-time buyers just like Ponzi schemes need new investors; without either, the value of the existing assets would collapse, revealing to all and sundry the dirty secret that kept both going. And that secret is the delusion we are sold about the need to buy housing, to own a 'home', to reap the benefits of forever-rising house prices, and so on. We are not only supposed to buy a house, we are also supposed to buy into the 'aspirational' myth that we are not proper adults, citizens, or whatever until we have that mortgage – "death contract" – tied around our throats. All we're doing by buying into both this delusion and myth, however, is joining the housing Ponzi scheme. Our grandparents, parents and their generation need us to join the housing market or the value of their house crashes, wiping out all that investment they've made in their property. Instead, think about other forms of housing like housing cooperatives or cohousing – whatever you do, avoid the housing ladder delusion.

Conclusion

It is important to note that we've all ended up tied into the assetization of our economies. We are now dependent on our housing, pensions, savings and insurance premiums for our standards of living. For all those now trying to enter the workforce, this connection has been loosened as their opportunities to acquire any of these are significantly reduced. The spectre of inter-generational clashes raises its head as boomers and X-ers, sitting pretty, are reliant on millenials buying into the same societal messages they bought into years ago. However, things have changed, not least of which is rising employment insecurity, debt servitude and exclusion from property ownership for most millenials. What is more, you have become increasingly dependent on your parents to support your decisions, your choices and your dreams as they are the ones who can finance these things.

This inter-generational inequality should not distract us from the wider systemic consequences of the dominance of large corporations, financial institutions and the inequalities we can see around us. We still need to face it, however. My parent's generation, my own generation and the next generation are all tied together by our current financial system, but in very different ways. The system benefits not only the top 1% but the rest of us to varying degrees. What this means for solidarity across the generations is critical. It might explain why things like the Occupy Movement and *Global May Manifesto*,[38] which represent a laudable attempt to formulate an egalitarian, progressive and ultimately optimistic vision of future politics and economic structures, inevitably raise hackles and engender criticism for its idealism even in supposedly liberal circles — see the comments section in *The Guardian* for example. Changing the current financial system poses real threats to all sorts of people, not just the top 1%. For example, if you want to change things it will probably mean ending the housing obsession, it will probably mean reforming pensions, it will probably mean higher taxes, and it will probably mean lots of things that have become unpalatable to the dominant narrative of ever-rising asset values and rising wealth. But, at heart, what it means is that we have to separate our interests from those of the top 1%, and we have to do it actively and concertedly because no one else will do it for us.

What critics of the Occupy Movement do highlight is the need for future generations to go beyond creating a list of "wants" and "demands". Instead you have to set in train concrete actions that will change the world. It's not about asking someone else for something or demanding they give up what they have, it's about changing your expectations, desires and choices in order to make what you want happen. You should be telling the rest of the world that you no longer want to sustain the collective delusions that brought us to the brink of financial collapse; rather, you want to remake the financial system by moving your position within it, whatever that may be.[39] More simply, it should say 'we will not pay the interest you need to maintain your economic system'. Just say no to paying interest!

Chapter 5. Manifesto for a Doomed Youth

1. Worth, O. (2013) *Resistance in the Age of Austerity*. London: Zed Books.
2. See Zero Hedge blog post (3 May 2012), available online: http://www.zerohedge.com/news/mystery-trader-revealed-and-his-name-hope.
3. See, https://www.youtube.com/watch?v=B6loH9P4-B8
4. It's probably worth highlighting the Citi Group "Plutonomy Reports" here. They note that "the world is dividing into two blocs - the plutonomies, where economic growth is powered by and largely consumed by the wealthy few, and the rest" (p.1, Equity Strategy memo), available online: http://our99angrypercent.wordpress.com/2011/11/27/download-citigroup-plutonomy-memos/
5. See, Bailey, J., Coward, J. and Whittaker, M. (2011) *Painful Separation*. London: Resolution Foundation, p.13.
6. Palma, J. (2009) The revenge of the market on the rentiers: Why neo-liberal reports of the end of history turned out to be premature. *Cambridge Journal of Economics* 33: p.842.
7. Harvey, D. (2005) A Brief History of Neoliberalism. Oxford: Oxford University Press, p.25.
8. Harvey, D. (2010) *The Enigma of Capital and the Crises of Capitalism*. Profile Books.
9. Notably, however, the expansion of personalized social insurance is evident well before the rise of the likes of Thatcher – see Coakley, J. and Harris, L. (1983) *City of Capital*. Oxford: Blackwell. There was a significant expansion of financial assets by British institutional investors during the 1960s and 1970s. For example, between 1957 and 1981 the total assets held by British institutional investors rose from £8.2 billion to £154.2 billion, the most significant rise happening during the 1970s as total assets went from £24.2 billion in 1967 to £105 billion in 1979 – a fourfold increase (p.96).
10. Francis, M. (2012) "A Crusade To Enfranchise The Many":

Thatcherism and the Property-Owning Democracy. *Twentieth Century British History* 23(2): 275-297.

11 Watson, M. (2010) House Price Keynesianism and the Contradictions of the Modern Investor Subject. *Housing Studies* 25(3); and, Crouch, C. (2011) *The Strange Non-Death of Neoliberalism*. Cambridge: Polity.

12 Walks, A. (2010) Bailing Out the Wealthy: Responses to the Financial Crisis, Ponzi Neoliberalism, and the City. *Human Geography*. 3 (3): p.64.

13 Mankiw, G. (2013) Defending the One Percent. *Journal of Economic Perspectives*, available online: http://scholar.harvard.edu/files/mankiw/files/defending_the_one_percent_0.pdf

14 Lanchester, J. (2010) *IOU*. Toronto: McClelland and Stewart, p.220.

15 Erturk, I., Froud, J., Johal, S., Leaver, A. and Williams, K. (eds) (2008) *Financialization at Work: Key Texts and Commentary*. London: Routledge.

16 Not the film-maker! Jackson, P. (2009) The Size and Scope of the Public Sector: An International Comparison, in T. Bovaird and E. Loffler (eds) *Public Sector Management Handbook* (2nd Edition). London: Routledge, pp.32-4.

17 Loomis, E. (2012) 8 Ways America's Headed Back to the Rober-Baron Era. *AlterNet* (2 July), available online: http://www.alternet.org/story/156111/8_ways_america%27s_headed_back_to_the_robber-baron_era

18 Mendelson, R. (2011) Canada Income Inequality. *The Huffington Post* (21 November), available online: http://www.huffingtonpost.ca/2011/11/21/canada-income-inequality-house-prices_n_1101655.html

19 Blyth, M. (2013) *Austerity*. Oxford: Oxford University Press, p.232.

20 Greider, W. 1987. *Secrets of the Temple: How the Federal Reserve Runs the Country*. Simon & Schuster.

Chapter 5. Manifesto for a Doomed Youth

21 Graeber, D. (2011) *Debt*. New York: Melville House
22 This article is a must read for anyone wondering about what the next 50 years could be like; McKibben, B. (2012) Global Warming's Terrifying New Math. *Rolling Stone* (19 July), available online: http://www.rollingstone.com/politics/news/global-warmings-terrifying-new-math-20120719
23 Collini, S. (2010) Browne's Gamble. *London Review of Books* 32(21): 23-25, available online: http://www.lrb.co.uk/v32/n21/stefan-collini/brownes-gamble; and Collini, S. (2011) From Robbins to McKinsey. *London Review of Books* 33(16) 9-14, available online: http://www.lrb.co.uk/v33/n16/stefan-collini/from-robbins-to-mckinsey
24 Martin, A. (2012) Slowly, as Student Debt Rises, Colleges Confront Costs. *New York Times* (14 May), available online: http://www.nytimes.com/2012/05/15/business/colleges-begin-to-confront-higher-costs-and-students-debt.html?_r=2&; and, *Globe and Mail* (2013) Education: Best of the Series, available online: http://www.theglobeandmail.com/news/national/time-to-lead/education-best-of-the-series/article6910463/
25 Cauchon, D. (2011) Students loans outstanding will exceed $1 trillion this year. *USA Today* (25 October), available online: http://usatoday30.usatoday.com/money/perfi/college/story/2011-10-19/student-loan-debt/50818676/1
26 Khimm, S. (2013) At the deadline: Student loan rates set to double. *MSNBC* (26 June), available online: http://tv.msnbc.com/2013/06/26/time-running-out-before-student-loan-rates-double/
27 Chakrabortty, A. (2013) Raise interest rates on old student loans, secret report proposes. *The Guardian* (13 June), available online: http://www.guardian.co.uk/money/2013/jun/13/raise-interest-rate-student-loans-secret-report
28 Antonova, A. (2012) Saddled with student debt? Welcome to America's screwed generation. *The Guardian* (1 August),

available online: http://www.guardian.co.uk/comment-isfree/2012/aug/01/student-debt-america-screwed-generation; Maisano, C. (2012) The Soul of Student Debt. *Jacobin* 9, available online: http://jacobinmag.com/2012/12/the-soul-of-student-debt/; and Williams, J. (2012) Occupying Student Debt. *Dissent* (30 January), available online: http://www.dissentmagazine.org/blog/occupying-student-debt

29 Kendzior, S. (2013) The millennial parent. *Al-Jazeera English* (29 May), available online: http://www.aljazeera.com/indepth/opinion/2013/05/20135296372576387.html; and Bakkila, S. (2013) Why You Should Never Have Taken that Prestigious Internship [interview with Sarah Kendzior]. *PolicyMic* website (14 June), available online: http://www.policymic.com/articles/48829/why-you-should-never-have-taken-that-prestigious-internship

30 Kendzior, S. (2013) Meritocracy for sale. *Al-Jazeera English* (4 May), available online: http://www.aljazeera.com/indepth/opinion/2013/05/20135371732699158.html;

31 Caon, V. (2012) Europe's lost generation: How it feels to be young and struggling in the EU. *The Guardian* (28 January), available online: http://www.guardian.co.uk/world/2012/jan/28/europes-lost-generation-young-eu

32 Pennycook, M., Cory, G. and Alakeson, V. (2013) *A Matter of Time: The rise of zero-hours contracts*. London: Resolution Foundation, available online: http://www.resolutionfoundation.org/publications/matter-time-rise-zero-hours-contracts/

33 Zero Hedge website (2013) *15 Signs that the Quality of Jobs in America is Fading Fast* (7 July), available online: http://www.zerohedge.com/news/2013-07-07/15-signs-quality-jobs-america-fading-fast

34 Boutang, Y.M. (2011) *Cognitive Capitalism*, Cambridge: Polity; Lazarrato, M. (1997) *Lavoro Immateriale e Soggettivita*. Verona: Ombre corte; and, Morini, C. and Fumagalli, A.

(2010) Life put to work: Towards a life theory of value. *ephemera*, 10(3/4): 234-255.
35   Walks, 'Bailing out the wealthy', note xii.
36   Blyth, *Austerity*, note xix.
37   Walks, A. (2012) Canada's housing bubble story: Mortgage securitization, the state, and the global financial crisis. *International Journal of Urban and Regional Research*, available online: http://onlinelibrary.wiley.com/doi/10.1111/j.1468-2427.2012.01184.x/abstract
38   Occupy Wall Street website (2012) *International Assembly: Global May Manifesto* (11 May), available online: http://occupywallst.org/article/international-assembly-globay-may/
39   For some interesting suggestions and information, see Scott, B. (2013) *The Heretic's Guide to Global Finance: Hacking the Future of Money*. London: Pluto Press.

Conclusion

While this may be the conclusion to the book, I don't intend to do much more than summarize what I've talked about in earlier chapters. I'm not really going to go into the implications of my arguments since I've tried to do this as I went and because my aim was to address the main policy or practical implications in Chapter 5. That being said, I do want to address one important question here; if we have not been neoliberal, does that mean we are heading that direction now?

As the effects of the global financial crisis (GFC) and its aftermath (e.g. recession, public debt and austerity) have rolled-out around the world, its impact has been highly uneven. It started with a liquidity crisis in the Atlantic Heartland, especially in the USA and UK, as financial institutions stopped lending to each another and anyone else, and then it mutated into a recession as the impacts of financial retrenchment were felt across other sectors of the economy. As unemployment rose, tax takes fell and governments bailed out sector after sector – first the banks then manufacturing – leading to a public debt crisis as government spending hit new heights, although not heights we've never seen before. In early 2010 this took a turn for the worse in Europe as, one after another, countries like Portugal, Ireland, Italy, Greece and Spain (the so-called PIIGS) faced sharp rises in the costs of government borrowing.

What we are left with now is an *austerity crisis* – the Coalition government in the UK, for example, has based its political survival on the pursuit of government cost-cutting in the face of continued recession and weak growth.[1] Other governments around the world have adopted similar austerity policies to combat rising borrowing costs and reduce their public debt, even though the underpinning arguments behind austerity are largely nonsense according to Mark Blyth.[2] Recently, one of the key economic rationales for austerity, a 2010 paper by Carmen Reinhart and Kenneth Rogoff, turned out to contain serious errors, all based on a simple spreadsheet error.[3] Whether this sort of thing will actually change government policies is something we have to wait and see, but maybe we shouldn't hold our breath.

A Summary of the Main Arguments

Put simply, the starting point for this book was that much of the literature and debate about neoliberalism has missed, ignored or misunderstood the importance of corporations, and other business organizations, in the economy. This is a huge gap in our knowledge of political-economic transformation, not only since the 1970s but going back to WW2 and even beforehand. While most people would recognize the dominant role of multinational corporations (MNCs) in the global economy, this is often hidden behind the ideological idolization and valorization of *free markets* as the most efficient, the most ethical and the most suitable mechanism for organizing our economies, our governments and even our personal behaviour. Now, there is no doubt that 'free' market ideologies are all around us, especially in the words of our politicians, business-people, media commentators and academics, but if we look closely at these words and what people actually do it is obvious that there is a major disconnect. We don't live in a free market society, let alone a neoliberal one where the market mechanism has replaced every other social institution. Social hierarchy, prejudice and discrimination of all stripes still leave their marks on us in our daily lives.

Returning to the main reason behind this book, it starts with Geoffrey Hodgson's argument that most economic activity actually takes place *inside* economic organizations and not *within* markets.[4] This is a crucial point when we discuss neoliberalism, yet isn't really considered by critical thinkers – with a few exceptions.[5] What Hodgson argues is that things like long-term employment contracts, fixed capital (e.g. machinery, buildings, etc.) spending, internal supply chains, etc. don't involve the market price mechanism; that is, they are a stable cost rather than a cost reflecting constantly changing market prices (e.g. businesses do not hire their workers each day, they hire them on long-term contracts). If we accept Hodgson's claim – and there doesn't seem much reason not to – that most economic activity takes place inside business organizations and not on markets, then several things follow from this.

First, over the 20th century the level of economic activity undertaken within business organizations, especially MNCs, has increased and in no way decreased; for example, since WW2 foreign direct investment (FDI) has increased significantly faster than international trade resulting in the emergence of MNCs with operations in many different parts of the world.[6] Second, this has meant that the role of markets has gradually eroded as economic activity is increasingly undertaken within business organizations (and not between them) leading to the rise of corporate monopolies – not only visible ones like Microsoft, but also invisible ones like the major suppliers that Barry C. Lynn talks about in his book *Cornered*.[7] Third, this raises an important point about business outsourcing; even though outsourcing has increased, all it has done is create systemic and interdependent contractual relations rather than market ones. To illustrate this point, all we need to think about are the global supply chains of corporations like Wal-Mart to realize that these are not 'market' relationships – they are about the power of a major buyer to enforce their demands on their weaker suppliers.[8] Fourth, even financial relations (e.g. borrowing and lending of money), which have also grown enormously in the last half of the 20th century, are not about promoting market relations; they are, rather, about reducing market uncertainty and market competition by insuring against loss via hedging, derivatives, and so on.[9] What all of this implies is that capitalism since WW2, whether we want to call it

Keynesian, neoliberal or something else, has been about avoiding and not encouraging market-like rule.

So, this is why I called this book "we have never been neoliberal". I've basically tried to show that we are not and have not been neoliberal if by neoliberal we mean the emergence and extension of market-like rule or market ethic. Instead, what has really characterized the last few decades are rationalities, ideas, policies and processes that have been about *freeing-the-monopolies*, not promoting free markets. In Chapter 1, for example, I highlighted how there are different schools of neoliberalism which don't necessarily share common perspectives, or rationalities in Michel Foucault's terms. Where this is most obvious is in the evolution of attitudes to corporate monopoly; originally, many neoliberal thinkers – e.g. Hayek, von Mises, Ropke, Friedman, Robbins, etc. – held strong and negative views about such economic monopolies. However, this changed with the second Chicago school as scholars like Friedman, Stigler and Director committed an about face and came to support corporate monopoly by arguing that it's efficient in consumer welfare terms. Now, my argument is that the rise of the second Chicago school as a site of policy influence is tied into its support for corporate monopoly; however, these Chicago neoliberals didn't *drive* the policy agenda, they merely tagged on, limpet-like, to the way things were going anyway. In this sense, they were nothing more than lapdogs to corporate power.

While I dug through the detritus of neoliberal thinking in Chapter 1, what I did in Chapter 2 was show how specific neoliberal ideas – in this case monetarism and fiscal prudence – were failures when politicians and policy-makers attempted to implement them. Monetarism failed in the USA and UK, for example, because the monetary aggregates kept on changing, which was unexpected and not predicted in theory. Ultimately the Reagan and Thatcher administrations were forced to borrow more as a consequence of the need to raise interest rates to counter inflation. My argument is that the supposedly neoliberal ideas, when enacted, led to contradictory outcomes, namely rising public debt as real interest rates rose in the 1980s. In large part this failure of neoliberal ideas, especially monetarism, resulted from the emergence of state-less financial markets (i.e. Euromarkets) which enabled private banks to take control of the money supply leaving governments in a financial straitjacket.

What the discussion of neoliberal ideas illustrates is that they are often not reflected in concrete policies or practices. Chapter 3 provides a clear example of this by focusing on the idea that financialization and neoliberalism are two-sides of a political-economic project to the restore power of economic elites – see David Harvey's work for an example of this perspective.[10] What I showed in this chapter is that such class-based analyses are too one-dimensional; they miss the important organizational changes that happened as well, especially the expansion of large, monopolistic corporations. As corporate monopolies have come to dominate our economies, they have been roundly cheered on by supposedly neoliberal thinkers who reversed their criticism of corporate monopoly. As a consequence we ended up with banks and other financial institutions that were *too-big-to-fail*, a seeming contradiction between (neoliberal) market-based policies and the long-standing growth of corporate monopolies and the concentration of economic power since at least the 1950s.

The concentration of financial assets I discussed at the end of Chapter 3 led me to my arguments in Chapter 4, which focused on the conceptualization of neoliberalism as a process – see, for example, Jamie Peck and Adam Tickell's work.[11] Again, these critical scholars miss the organizational dimensions of recent political-economic change, what I've defined as *assetization* but basically concern the expansion of corporations and how their assets are governed. What I showed is that the concentration of economic power is tied to corporate restructuring as intangible asset values came to legitimate rising share prices. What has happened is that the ownership of publicly listed corporations and their assets has shifted from individuals to a few institutional investors who now control at least 60% of corporate shares and probably more. There are two implications of this shift: first, institutional investors are not competing against each other because if they did their financial assets (e.g. shares) would drop in value; and second, this concentration of financial assets has led to a systemic interdependence between corporations, institutional investors and individuals in which market competition becomes incredibly damaging. Hence, all players in the economy seek to avoid any interruption to rising asset values, of whatever sort (e.g. market, government, etc.).

I finished up my arguments in Chapter 5. I first discussed the outcomes of the changes I wrote about in the previous chapters and then outlined a manifesto for what I've termed the "doomed youth". I'm including all those people who entered or were about to enter the labour market at the start of the GFC and ever since. It's now a big age range, going from 16 years to 30 years old since the GFC, which began six years ago, is still going strong today. That's a lot of people who have been largely abandoned by mainstream politicians, policy-makers and decision-makers. What I suggested in this chapter is that there is a simple way to make their presence felt, one that will have an impact on politicians, businesses and the rest of us sitting pretty, and that is to stop paying interest. Whether that means reducing their consumer spending, not borrowing to go to university, abandoning attempts to get on the property ladder, or declaring bankruptcy is a decision they need to make. Since our asset-based economies are reliant on them buying into the Ponzi scheme that is the financial system, if they make this leap then they may bring the rest of us down with them. Maybe we deserve it ...

What if We are Seeing Neoliberalism Emerge Now?

This brings me to the final point I want to make in this book. As I said above, one question worth asking right now is; if we were and are not neoliberal, are we going to become neoliberal now as a result of the GFC? Several people have written about what comes after neoliberalism,[12] as they conceive it, but what might threaten to emerge over the next few years? Well, it's probably worth looking at what has happened since 2007 in order to answer this question.

One thing that strikes me is the lack of political will to take on big business, especially the banks that have played such a significant role in the crises so far. Whether or not they have been nationalized or bailed out or their assets guaranteed, the one thing that characterizes Wall Street, the City of London and probably every other centre of finance is the lack of self-awareness and self-reflection shown by the people running the show. It's almost as if people working in banks and other financial businesses can't see that their position is (inter-)dependent on the rest of the economy – as Matt Taibbi so vividly put it, "The worlds' most powerful investment bank [Goldman Sachs] is a great vampire squid wrapped around the face of humanity, relentlessly jamming its blood funnel into anything that smells like money".[13] We have trained cohorts of university graduates, spilling out of business schools with little else on their mind but pillaging the rest of us.[14] This has not stopped, no matter whether we now talk more about corporate social responsibility or sustainable business or banking reform. But, this is not the most worrying thing we might imagine in the future.

What if, accepting that neoliberalism hasn't taken over the world already, we then consider what happens if neoliberalism does actually take over the world now. What would the world look like if it was dominated by markets and not large corporations? The short answer is not better than now or the recent past. The possibility that most people will be left to compete against

Conclusion

one another for a dwindling number of jobs, personal assets (e.g. housing), individualized social insurance (e.g. pensions), and so on is frightening. I don't think it'll end this way, however. Instead, I'd like to end on a positive note and so will turn to Karl Polanyi for why things will work themselves out in some acceptable form.[15] He wrote about something he called the "double movement" which was the unconscious and unplanned popular response to the damage caused by unfettered capitalism. It's what we're seeing now in countries throughout the world, in the form of the Arab Spring, the Occupy Movement, the resistance to austerity in countries like Greece and Spain, and so on. What this offers is timely reminder to our rulers that people will only take so much shit before they revolt, and the amount of shit they are drowning in right now is too much. What has happened since 2007 has left us all with a nasty taste in our mouths and, hopefully, a desire to do something about it.

I want to end this book with a quote which I think helps to sum up what I'd like people to take away from this book. The quote comes from the comic *The Invisibles* by Grant Morrison:

> "We made gods and jailers because we felt small and alone ...
> We let them try us and judge us and, like lambs to the slaughter, we allowed ourselves to be ... *sentenced*.
> See! Now! Our sentence is up."

1. See, Kitson, M., Martin, R. and Tyler, P. (2011) The geographies of austerity. *Cambridge Journal of Regions, Economy and Society* 4: 289-302.
2. Blyth, M. (2013) *Austerity*. Oxford: Oxford University Press.
3. Gongloff, M. (2013) Reinhart And Rogoff's Pro-Austerity Research Now Even More Thoroughly Debunked By Studies. *The Huffington Post Canada* (30 May), available online: http://www.huffingtonpost.com/2013/05/30/reinhar

t-rogoff-debunked_n_3361299.html

4 Hodgson, G. (2005) Knowledge at work: Some neoliberal anachronisms. Review of Social Economy 63(4): 547-565.

5 For example, Crouch, C. (2011) *The Strange Non-Death of Neoliberalism*. Cambridge: Polity.

6 Dicken, P. (2011) *Global Shift*. Guildford Press.

7 Lynn, B.C. (2010) *Cornered*. New Jersey: John Wiley & Sons.

8 Fishman, C. (2006) *Wal-Mart*. London: Penguin Books.

9 Scott, B. (2013) *The Heretic's Guide to Global Finance: Hacking the Future of Money*. London: Pluto Press.

10 See Harvey, D. (2005) A Brief History of Neoliberalism. Oxford: Oxford University Press; and, Harvey, D. (2010) *The Enigma of Capital and the Crises of Capitalism*. London: Profile Books.

11 Peck, J. and Tickell, A. (2002) Neoliberalizing space. *Antipode* 34(3): 380-404; and, Tickell, A. and Peck, J. (2003) Making global rules: globalisation or neoliberalization, in J. Peck and H. Yeung (eds) *Remaking the global economy*. London: Sage, pp.163-182.

12 A few examples include: Brenner, N., Peck, J. and Theodore, N. (2010) After neoliberalization? *Globalizations* 7(3): 327-345; Helleiner, E. (2010) A Bretton Woods moment? The 2007-2008 crisis and the future of global finance. *International Affairs* 86(3): 619-636; and, Hendrikse, R. and Sidaway, J. (2010) Commentary: Neoliberalism 3.0. *Environment and Planning A* 42: 2037-2042.

13 Taibbi, M. (2011) *Griftopia*. New York: Spiegel and Grau Trade Paperbacks, p.209.

14 See, Khurana, R. (2007) *From Higher Aims to Hired Hands: The Social Transformation of American Business Schools and the Unfulfilled Promise of Management as a Profession*. Princeton: Princeton University Press; and Fourcade, M. and Khurana, R. (2011) *From social control to financial economics: The linked ecologies of economics and business in twentieth century America*.

Harvard Business School Working Paper 11-071.
15   Polanyi, K. (1944[2001]) *The Great Transformation*. New York: Beacon,

zero books

Contemporary culture has eliminated both the concept of the public and the figure of the intellectual. Former public spaces – both physical and cultural – are now either derelict or colonized by advertising. A cretinous anti-intellectualism presides, cheerled by expensively educated hacks in the pay of multinational corporations who reassure their bored readers that there is no need to rouse themselves from their interpassive stupor. The informal censorship internalized and propagated by the cultural workers of late capitalism generates a banal conformity that the propaganda chiefs of Stalinism could only ever have dreamt of imposing. Zer0 Books knows that another kind of discourse – intellectual without being academic, popular without being populist – is not only possible: it is already flourishing, in the regions beyond the striplit malls of so-called mass media and the neurotically bureaucratic halls of the academy. Zer0 is committed to the idea of publishing as a making public of the intellectual. It is convinced that in the unthinking, blandly consensual culture in which we live, critical and engaged theoretical reflection is more important than ever before.